P9-CDH-710

THE MIND OF THE MASTER

The Mind of the Master

By John Watson, D.D.

(Ian Maclaren)

NEW YORK

DODD, MEAD AND COMPANY

1896

TO MY PEOPLE

IN GRATEFUL RECOGNITION

OF THEIR

CHARITY, LOYALTY, AND

PATIENCE

CONTENTS

JESUS OUR SUPREME TEACHER

I

JESUS OUR SUPREME TEACHER

When Jesus on one occasion strictly enjoined His disciples that they should not allow any of their number to usurp mastership over his brethren, and commanded them to acknowledge Him as the alone Lord of the conscience, it is evident that He had in His mind the intolerable bondage of thought into which the religious people of His day had fallen. His own disheartening experience as the chief of God's prophets lent a keen edge to His words, and are a complete illustration of their meaning.

No teacher ever gave such pledges of Divine authority as Jesus; no people could have been better prepared for His evangel than the Jews. They had been set apart as in a cloister that they might hear the Divine voice, and a succession of prophets had

come from the presence of God to declare the
Divine will. A nation had been trained in the
hope of the Messiah to wait for the dayspring
from on high and the fulness of God's kingdom. It might have been expected that this
well-tilled field would have been open soil for
Jesus' words, and one dares to believe that
there might have been an auspicious seedtime
had the Jews passed, say, from Isaiah to Jesus,
or had Jesus come while the glow of Daniel's
visions was still fresh.

Unfortunately between the last of the great
prophets and the advent of Jesus there came
in one of the secondary periods which follow
on an age of inspiration, when the intellectual
consciousness of a people, hitherto running full
and free, comes to a standstill and stagnates.
No teacher of the first order arose to continue
the stream of revelation, but in his place appeared that lower order of mind to which the
letter is everything, on which the Spirit never
breathes. The scribes sat in the seat of the
prophets, and revelation was succeeded by exposition. Under the hand of rabbis without
insight or imagination the life departed from
Hebrew thought, and nothing was left but

empty bloodless forms, as when a flower is plucked and dried. Theological pedantry had done its work in the days of Jesus, and had reduced the sublime ethics of the Old Testament to a wearisome absurdity. The beneficent law of rest, so full of sympathy with struggling people, was translated into a series of regulations of peddling detail and incredible childishness. The clean heart of the prophets sank into an endless washing of hands, and filial piety was wantonly outraged that the temple taxes might be swollen. Jewish faith had become a painted show, a husk in which the kernel had withered.

It is, on first thoughts, inexplicable that any body of religious people—and one must admit that the Jews were the most religious people on the face of the earth—should have refused the luminous and winsome teaching of Jesus, and actually sent Him to the Cross for His Evangel. When one thinks a little longer, and puts himself in the place of the contemporaries of Jesus, it comes home to him that they were not really able to receive the truth, and that he himself might, in the same circumstances, have condemned Jesus as a blasphemer. For the irresistible attraction of Jesus, as it now seems to us, was His reasonableness, and that was shown by His appeal at every turn to reality. 'This is what I say, and you will see that this is what ought to be,' was ever Jesus' argument; and to an honest mind, without bias or preoccupation, such a plea was unanswerable. But if the mind had long lost touch with truth at first hand, and was possessed by traditions about truth, then Jesus could have no access, and indeed might be only offensive. Jesus and the Jews were ever at cross purposes in this matter. He made His appeal past tradition to truth, and they disallowed this appeal and judged Him by tradition; and by this standard there can be no doubt He was a heretic.

Jesus' attitude to tradition was quite clear and consistent. It is not to be supposed that He denied the right or propriety of Jewish scholars studying and theorizing about the Old Testament Scriptures, for this were to cramp the just exercise of human reason. He would no doubt consider it a fitting tribute to revelation that earnest and able men should reason truth out into her farthest conclusions and lessons for the guidance both of conscience and intellect. As it happened, the work of a sterile age did not yield much either of light or strength to generations following. But that was its misfortune, not its crime; the rabbis so far were within their rights and their duty. Theology, either in the department of dogma or ethics, requires no justification; it only calls for limitation. As soon as they proposed to bind their results upon their fellow-men with authority, the scribes passed beyond their province and were guilty of treason against the free commonwealth of God's children. As dictators of faith and manners, Jesus resisted them without reserve or compromise, and forbade His followers to follow in their steps. The spiritual arrogance of the rabbis had been a blight on Judaism, and Jesus desired that His new religion should retain a perennial freshness. There was only one guarantee that Christianity would not share the same fate, and that was the continual return to Jesus.

When Jesus laid this injunction on His Apostles, He surely anticipated the history of His faith; and circumstances have justified His foresight. It is a necessity of the human mind to theorize about truth ; it is a calamity to substitute theories for truth. One almost despairs at times because we seem the victims of an irresistible tendency to ignore the real, and to be content with the artificial. No sooner has some man of genius painted a picture or conceived a poem, or even made a speech with moral intention, than people set themselves to invent amazing meanings and applications, and raise such a dust of controversy that the original effect is utterly lost. We are amused by the societies which are the custodians of Ruskin and Browning, but none can be indifferent to the manipulation of Jesus' words. If Jesus' delicate poetry be reduced to prose, and the fair, carved work of His parables be used for the building of prisons, and His lovely portrait of God be 'restored' with grotesque colouring, and His lucid principles of life be twisted into harassing regulations, then Jesus has been much wronged, and the world has suffered irreparable loss. This is the disaster Jesus dreaded, and no one will deny that it has, in some degree at least, come to pass.

The footsteps of the holy Apostles had not died away—concerning whose relation

to Jesus something will be said—before the
Fathers arose, and became, with the lapse of
time, lords of the Christian conscience. Great
theologians of the Middle Ages gradually took
rank with the Fathers, while council after council, from Nice to Trent, saddled their accumulated dogmas on the Church. Chief Reformers almost literally dictated creeds to nations,
and the pragmatical seventeenth century forged
a yoke of doctrines so minute, tedious, and unreasonable that it became too irksome even for
our more patient fathers. Every side of truth
and every rite of Jesus was turned into a test
by which honest-minded and simple-hearted
disciples of Jesus were tried, condemned, cast
out, burned. Unity was as much wanting as
charity, for Christians in the matter of creed
agreed in nothing except in ignoring the Gospels and persecuting one another. Romans
rest on the councils down to the one that affirmed the infallibility of the pope; an Anglican goes back to the early councils and the
Fathers; a Lutheran measures his faith by the
Confession of Augsburg; and the Scottish
Church seems to suppose that Christianity was
only once thoroughly understood, when an as-

sembly of English divines met at Westminster.
Bodies of Christian folk have also ignored
Jesus' warning against Rabbinism, and have
surrendered their birthright by allowing themselves to be called by the names of men, and
so we have Socinians, Wesleyans, Cameronians,
Morisonians, and what not. One denomina-
tion is called, with surely some slight want of
humour, if not of reverence, ' Lady Hunting-
don's Connection;' and so it is made evident
that a masterful woman can actually found a
Church and lay down a creed. It comes as a
shock on one to attend some heresy trial, and
hear the prosecution quoting a foreign divine
of almost miraculous woodenness and the de-
fendant taking refuge in a second-rate com-
mentator. If you were to ask, as is very natural, why neither will refer at once and finally
to the words of Jesus, who can hardly have
been silent on any point of importance, it would
be at once explained that such a reference is an
irrelevancy and a subterfuge; and one must admit that it would be an attempt to get behind
the rabbis to Jesus. But does it matter much
what any rabbi says? and is not the only vital
question, What saith the Master?

There are certain rights which are legal; there are certain rights which are natural. No law can take away the latter, nor can a man divest himself of them by any form of engagement; and among the inherent rights of a Christian man is his appeal to Jesus as the one Judge of truth. It has often lain dormant in the Church; it has at times been powerfully exercised. Some one discovers that the water of life is clearer and sweeter from the spring than in a cistern, and shows the grass-grown path to the spring. Perhaps there has been no long period without some voice summoning Christians to break away from the tyranny of tradition and return to the liberty of Jesus. This has been the work of all Reformers from Tauler to Luther, from Luther to Wesley—to unearth the evangel of Jesus from the mass of dogmas and rites which have overlaid it. Two parties have been in recurring conflict—the Traditionalists, who insist, 'This is what our fathers have said, and what you must believe;' and the Evangelists, who declare, 'This is what Jesus has said, and this only will we believe.' When Traditionalism has the upper hand, it burns its opponents, as the Roman Church did

John Huss, or annoys them, as the Church of England did Robertson of Brighton; when Evangelism is strong, it clears an open space where men can breathe and see Jesus. By-and-by each evangelical movement loses its free spirit, and settles down into a new form of traditionalism. Brave hands clear away the covering from the ancient temple of truth, and then the generation following allow the sand-drift to cover its columns once more. It is a long battle between a handful of faithful men and the desert, and too often the desert has won.

The spirit of our day is so resentful of traditionalism as to be even impatient of theology, which is foolish ; and to threaten faith, which would be ruin. No one, however, need be alarmed, for there is good reason to believe that the end will be the toleration of a noble science and the re-establishment of faith. When workmen come with pickaxe and shovel, it is either to destroy or to discover, and the aim of present thought is discovery. Were earnest men rebelling against ancient dogmas because they were an integral part of Jesus' teaching, this would be a very serious matter.

This would be nothing short of a deliberate attack on Jesus. If they be only endeavouring to correct the results of theological science by the actual teaching of Jesus, then surely nothing could be more hopeful. This must issue in the revival of Christianity. There is no question that for some time dogmatic theology has been at a discount. They say that both the Fathers and the Puritans are unsaleable, and this is to be regretted. But there can be little question that Biblical theology is at a premium, and this is of far more importance. Never have there been so many Lives of Jesus; never have His words been so anxiously studied. This is as it ought to be, and every Protestant may well lift up his head. For what did the Reformers of the sixteenth century contend, but the right of Christian men to build their faith at first hand on the words of Holy Scripture? We are living in a second Reformation, and it were an immense blunder for us to go back on the principle of all Reformations, and insist directly or indirectly that Protestant councils should come in between Christians and Christ. 'When I say the religion of Protestants,' wrote Chillingworth, 'I do not un-

derstand the doctrines of Luther, or Calvin, or
Melanchthon, nor the Confession of Augsburg
or Geneva, nor the Catechism of Heidelberg,
nor the Articles of the Church of England ;
no, nor the harmony of all Protestant Confes-
sions, but that wherein they all agree and
which they subscribe with a greater harmony
as the perfect rule of their faith and actions,
that is, the Bible.' Perhaps the ground principle of one Reformation was never more admirably stated : the principle of our Reformation
is an advance along the same line. The religion of Protestants, or let us say Christians, is
not the Bible in all its parts, but first of all that
portion which is its soul, by which the teaching of Prophets and Apostles must itself be
judged—the very words of Jesus.

As soon as any body of men band themselves
together for a common object—whether it be
making a railway or regenerating a world—
they must come to an understanding, and
promise loyalty. This is their covenant, which
no man need accept unless he please, but
which, after acceptance, he must keep. When
Jesus founded that unique society which He
called the Kingdom of God, and we prefer to

call the Church, it was necessary He should lay down its basis, and this is what He did in the Sermon on the Mount. For we ought not to think of that sermon as a mere detailed report of one of His numerous addresses, which often sprang from unexpected circumstances. It was not a defence against the Pharisee, like the 15th chapter of St. Luke, or an explanation to the disciples, like the 13th of St. Matthew. It was an elaborate and deliberate utterance, made by arrangement, and to a select audience. It was Christ's manifesto, and the constitution of Christianity. When Jesus opened His mouth, His new society was in the air. When He ceased, every one knew its nature, and also on what terms a man might belong to it. It would be very difficult to say which is the latest creed of Christianity—there is always some new one in formation, but there can be no question which is the oldest. Among all the creeds of Christendom the only one which has the authority of Christ Himself is the Sermon on the Mount. When one reads the Creed which was given by Jesus, and the Creeds which have been made by Christians, he cannot fail to detect an immense difference, and it does not matter whether he selects the Nicene Creed or the Westminster Confession. They all have a family likeness to each other, and a family unlikeness to the Sermon on the Mount. They deal with different subjects, they move in a different atmosphere. Were the Athanasian Creed and the Beatitudes printed in parallel columns, one would find it hard to believe that both documents were virtually intended to serve the same end, to be a basis of discipleship. It is not that they vary in details, insisting on different points of one consistent covenant, but that they are constructed on different principles. When one asks, 'What is a Christian?' the Creeds and the Sermon not only do not give the same answer, but models so contradictory that from the successive specifications he could create two types without any apparent resemblance. We all must know many persons who would pass as good Christians by the Sermon, and be cast out by the Creeds, and many to whom the Creeds are a broad way and the Sermon is a very strait gate. Since there is nothing we ought to be more anxious about than being true Christians, there is nothing we ought to think out more carefully than this startling variety.

What must strike every person about Jesus' sermon is that it is not metaphysical but ethical. What He lays stress upon are such points as these: the Fatherhood of God over the human family; His perpetual and beneficent providence for all His children; the excellence of simple trust in God over the earthly care of this world; the obligation of God's children to be like their Father in heaven; the paramount importance of true and holy motives; the worthlessness of a merely formal righteousness; the inestimable value of heart righteousness; forgiveness of sins dependent on our forgiving our neighbour; the fulfilling of the law, and the play of the tender and passive virtues. Upon the man who desired to be His disciple and a member of God's Kingdom were laid the conditions of a pure heart, of a forgiving spirit, of a helpful hand, of a heavenly purpose, of an unworldly mind. Christ did not ground His Christianity in thinking, or in doing, but first of all in being. It consisted in a certain type of soul—a spiritual shape of the inner self. Was a man satisfied with this type, and would

B

he aim at it in his own life? Would he put his name to the Sermon on the Mount, and place himself under Jesus' charge for its accomplishment? Then he was a Christian according to the conditions laid down by Jesus in the fresh daybreak of His religion.

When one turns to the Creeds, the situation has changed, and he finds himself in another world. They have nothing to do with character; they do not afford an idea of character; they do not ask pledges of character; they have no place in their construction for character. From their first word to the last they are physical or metaphysical, not ethical. They dwell on the relation of the three Persons in the Holy Trinity; the Divine and human natures in the Person of Jesus; His miraculous birth through the power of the Holy Ghost; the connection between His sacrifice and the Divine law; the nature of the penalty He paid, and its reference to His Atonement; the purposes of God regarding the salvation of individuals, and the collision between human Will and Divine; the means by which grace is conveyed to the soul; the mystery of the sacraments, and the intermediate state.

From time to time those problems have been discussed, and the conclusions of the majority formed into dogmas which have been made the test of Christianity. If any person should decline assent to one or all of those propositions, as the case may be,—on the ground that he does not understand them, for instance,—and offers instead adherence to Jesus' Creed in the Sermon on the Mount, it would be thought to be beside the question ; just as if any one had declined obedience to Jesus' commandments, and offered instead acceptance of some theory of His Person, the Master would have refused His discipleship with grave emphasis.

It may, of course, be urged that Jesus said many things afterwards which must be added to the Sermon on the Mount, to form the complete basis of Christian discipleship, and that great discourse is sometimes belittled as an elementary utterance, to which comparatively slight importance should now be attached. Certainly Jesus did expound and amplify the principles of His first deliverance, but there is no evidence that He altered the constitution of His Kingdom either by imposing fresh conditions or omitting the old. Did He not teach on to

the Cross that we stood to God as children to
a Father, and must do His will: that for no sin
was there or could there be forgiveness till it
was abandoned ; that the state of the soul and
not the mere outside life was everything; that
the sacrifice of self, and not self-aggrandisement
was His method of salvation ; that love was life ?
And when He said,—' Believe in Me ; carry My
Cross,' was He not calling men to fulfil His Gospel ?   If one had come to Christ at Capernaum
or Jerusalem, and said, ' Master, there is nothing I so desire as to keep Thy sayings.   Wilt
Thou have me, weak and ignorant although I
be, as Thy disciple ? ' can you imagine Christ
then, or now, or at any time interposing with
a series of doctrinal tests regarding either the
being of God or the history of man ?   It is impossible because it would be incongruous.   Indeed if Christ did revise and improve the conditions of discipleship, we should learn that
from the last address in the upper room.   But
what was the obligation He then laid on the
disciples' conscience, as with His dying breath ?
' This is My commandment, that ye love one
another as I have loved you.'   It is the Sermon
on the Mount in brief.

No church since the early centuries has had the courage to formulate an ethical creed, for even those bodies of Christians which have no written theological creeds, yet have implicit affirmations or denials of doctrine as their basis. Imagine a body of Christians who should take their stand on the sermon of Jesus, and conceive their creed on His lines. Imagine how it would read, 'I believe in the Fatherhood of God; I believe in the words of Jesus; I believe in the clean heart; I believe in the service of love; I believe in the unworldly life; I believe in the Beatitudes; I promise to trust God and follow Christ, to forgive my enemies and to seek after the righteousness of God.' Could any form of words be more elevated, more persuasive, more alluring? Do they not thrill the heart and strengthen the conscience? Liberty of thought is allowed; liberty of sinning is alone denied. Who would refuse to sign this creed? They would come from the east, and the west, and the north, and the south to its call, and even they who would hesitate to bind themselves to a crusade so arduous would admire it, and long to be worthy. Does one say this is too ideal, too unpractical, too quixotic? That no church could stand and work on such a basis? For three too short years the Church of Christ had none else, and it was by holy living, and not by any metaphysical subtleties, the Primitive Church lived, and suffered, and conquered.

THE DEVELOPMENT OF TRUTH

II

THE DEVELOPMENT OF TRUTH

Certain ancient and mystical theologians used to divide the history of revelation into three dispensations. One lasted from Abraham to John Baptist, the dispensation of the Father; another from Christ's Baptism to His Ascension, the dispensation of the Son; from Pentecost to Christ's Second Coming, the dispensation of the Holy Ghost. Beneath this fantastic language lay an accurate idea of the development of truth. First of all some one more receptive and imaginative than his fellows is haunted by the conviction that God must be One, and sets out in the great quest. He dies and leaves the legacy of his faith to the generation following. Some kindred spirit receives the torch and blows it into flame, and so the knowledge of God grows till men make Him the strength of their life. This is the age of discovery. At last a man appears on earth who realises all that saints have longed for and prophets have foretold, from Whose face God looks, through Whose will God speaks, beyond Whom no clearer revelation can be expected or imagined. This is the age of possession. Lastly comes the long aftertime when men begin slowly to understand what they have received, and make it their own. This is the age of assimilation. Isaiah looked forward and anticipated Christ, St. John saw Jesus and laid his head on the Master's bosom. We hold Jesus' words and life in our hands; we are learning what He intended and what He was. We live, therefore, in a very true sense, in the dispensation of His spirit.

Whatever words be used to distinguish the three periods, it seems at least clear that the teaching of Jesus must have an especial value and authority, and it is at least likely that the other two periods will be subordinate. Jesus delivered Himself on this important matter before He departed, and as once He claimed the authority of Master when He said, 'One is Master, even Christ,' so He now claimed the monopoly of truth by such a passage as this:

'Howbeit when He the spirit of truth is come, He will guide you into all *the* truth; for He shall not speak of Himself, but whatsoever He shall hear that shall He speak, and He will show you things to come. He shall glorify me; for He shall receive of Mine and shall show it unto you.' Again Jesus said, 'The Comforter, which is the Holy Ghost, whom the Father will send in my name, He shall teach you all things and bring all things to your remembrance whatsoever I have said unto you.' And once more, 'Henceforth I call you not servants; for the servant knoweth not what his lord doeth: but I have called you friends; for all things that I have heard of my Father I have made known unto you.' This may be accepted as Jesus' deliverance on the development of truth, and the statement of His relation to His Apostles.

One notices in the face of the words that Jesus makes a most distinct and also a most guarded claim as the prophet of God. He does not assert that He has compassed the length and breadth of human knowledge. Vast domains were left untouched by Jesus, and anyone who goes to our Master for instruction, say in science or philosophy, can only be disappointed. His sphere was religion—the character of God, the principles of the spiritual life, the forgiveness of sins, the discipline of the soul, the life to come. Those are the themes of Jesus, and on them He has said the last word. He cleansed away the mists that hung round the loftiest reaches of truth, and has made plain the soul's way unto God. No one can deny that Jesus has given to mankind what deserves to be called the truth.

Nor does Jesus mean to say that He has instructed His disciples fully in the truth, for this has been an impossibility. Within three years He could not follow out to its conclusions the revelation He made of God and man, nor apply His laws to every side of human life. His service was to lay down the infallible principles on which we could think rightly on religion. They can be all found in the gospels; they lie to any man's hand. Jesus gave the few axioms of the spiritual science on which its whole reasoning can be surely built. He placed us in possession of the mine, leaving the ages to mint its contents and make the gold current coin. Within the same discourse Jesus assures His disciples that He had told them everything He knew, and also that there were many more things that they were not yet able to receive which He would tell them afterwards.

When Jesus explained that He had kept nothing back, and yet had much more to give, He was not contradicting Himself, but only distinguishing between the substance and the development of truth. One might say with perfect accuracy that a seed contains the plant, stem, ears and full corn, and that when one gives the seed he gives all. Yet this is not the denial of the spring, and the summer, and the autumn time. After the same fashion it may be truly said that if any speaker should sow a living idea in the mind of a receptive hearer, and that idea were afterwards cast into various forms and carried into great actions, both words and deeds could be assigned to the original giver. The germ has the potency, it has also the very shape of all the coming life. Whatever, therefore, is said by St. Paul or St. John, by Augustine or Clement, so far as it conforms to type, may be assigned to Jesus, so that while He said little, if one goes by volume of speech, and wrote nothing, He has been speaking in every after age where any disciple has thought according to His mind. So it was right to say that Jesus gave the Evangel with His own lips, to say also that the Evangel has been continued by Him through other lips unto this present.

What has to be laid down in the strongest terms and held in perpetual remembrance is that Jesus gave in substance final truth, and that no one, apostle or saint, could or did add anything to the original deposit, however much he might expound or enforce it. This is the only position which secures a consistent and authoritative standard by which later teaching can be judged, and, apart from Jesus' own words, it is established by two arguments. One is probability or the fitness of things. Is it likely that Jesus who came to declare the Divine Will and reveal the Father would leave any truth of the first magnitude to be told by His servants? It is to be expected that prophets should anticipate Jesus' gospel and that apostles should apply it; but it were amazing if either should supplement Jesus. When any person imagines revelation in Holy Scripture as a level plain wherein Abraham or St. Paul stand as high as Jesus, he gives one pause; when any person conceives of revelation as an ascending scale, wherein the apostles stand above Jesus, he astounds one. If it be not an impiety, it is surely an extravagance.

Perhaps the argument from fact may be still more conclusive, and can be very easily grasped. It has happened that certain doctrines of theology have aroused fierce repugnance, and have been a grievous stumblingblock to faith. Most people have accepted them against the instincts of the heart and the light of reason, because the alternative seemed to be the refusal of Christianity. Many people have abandoned the religion of Jesus because they could not accept even its blessing with monstrous views of God annexed. Both classes would have found vast relief if they had only examined the quarter from which the texts in favour of those doctrines were drawn. Doctrines of reprobation may have some slight support in passages, for instance, of the Old Testament and Epistles, wrested for the most part from the context and general spirit of the writer, but they have none in the discourses of Jesus. They are ideas out of the line of Jesus' thought, branches tied on to the vine, withering and ready for the burning. One may accept it as a rule that the doctrines which rest on the gospels are reasonable, and are living, and that the doctrines which have no support in the gospels are less than reasonable and are dying, which surely goes far to show that Jesus' words are the truth.

There was a day, to illustrate this point from ethics, when good people defended slavery from the Book, and were understood to make out a strong case. Certainly they did find many passages in their support, and made fine play with St. Paul's Epistle to Philemon. No Christian man now believes that a word can be said for slavery. No one now would be moved by a hundred texts in its favour. Slavery has been condemned both by the spirit and by the teaching of Jesus. When He taught the Fatherhood of God, the brotherhood of man followed, and the end of slavery became a matter of time. It is growing clearer that many doctrines of Christian men are not lasting, but that every word of Jesus is eternal.

It has been urged that Jesus was unable to give certain truths of the first order to His dis-

ciples, because they would have been before
the event and therefore unintelligible at the
time. Their statement had to be left to the
apostles, and without St. Paul we had not
possessed to-day a complete gospel. If there
be two truths of this kind, surely they are the
sacrifice of Jesus and the presence of the Holy
Ghost. How could Jesus expound His death
before He died, and explain the indwelling of
His Spirit before He came? As it was, however, Jesus did refer to His death, its purpose
and effect, in images so lucid and convincing
that they admit of no improvement. After all
the reasoning of the Epistle to the Romans
one still turns to the incident of Zaccheus and
the utterance of Jesus with great and final satisfaction. When Jesus declared that He had
come to lay down His life a ransom for many,
and that in order every one might understand
in what sense He ransomed men from their sins,
took the salvation of Zaccheus as an illustration, one understands the atonement. St.
Paul has touched excellently in various letters
on the work of the Holy Spirit, and his words
have fed many, but all the words that ever
came from that inspired man are not to be

C

compared with the promise of the Comforter given in the upper room.

When one affirms the subordination of the Old Testament Scriptures to the Gospels it sounds a commonplace, and is indeed only a reminder of an obvious fact. The thought of the Old Testament moves forward to the life of Jesus. Its conduct is revised by the commandments of Jesus; its piety is crowned in Jesus' last discourses. We read the 53rd chapter of Isaiah in order that we may visit Calvary. The Ten Words are only eclipsed by the Law of Love. There is one passage dearer than the 23rd Psalm, and that is the 14th chapter of St. John's Gospel. The faith that would seek its guidance from the Patriarchs rather than from the Apostles, and quotes from its history to qualify the Gospels, is elementary and undeveloped. The massacre of the Canaanites may have been a little better in its purpose than the morals of the day; but it is an impossible action for any Christian, and the idea of the Messiah as the head of a righteous Jewish state was a noble dream eight hundred years before Christ, but something less than the kingdom of God. One part of the Old Testament is Christian in spirit and intention,—that is justified and remains, receiving new life from Jesus. One part is less than Christian—that is abrogated and disappears—replaced by Jesus.

The relation of the Apostles to Jesus is a question of much greater difficulty, and demands very careful treatment. When any one writes as if St. Paul were in the affair of teaching not only the equal of Jesus, but His superior—giving to the world more precious truth than the Gospels,—he has surely somewhat failed in reverence for the Master. When some other writer feels himself able to correct the Apostles with a light mind, as if they were ordinary theologians, he may fairly be charged with disrespect for the Master's chief servants. It is exasperating to be offered a choice between accepting the Gospel of St. Luke, with its three great parables of Jesus, and the 1st Epistle to the Corinthians, with its ascetical treatment of marriage, as of exactly the same authority for faith and marriage, or reducing St. Paul to the level of Tertullian or Calvin. One is haunted with the idea, as he reads both the Old and the New Testaments, that there must be a centre from which this varied litera-

ture can be judged,—a Master whom its writers
acknowledged—to whom they approximate.
As there have been centuries of the past when
art reached a lovely perfection—never again
approached—so there have also been centuries
when religion was touched by the Divine
Spirit. The fifth century before Christ was
such an one in Greece, when the Parthenon
was built : the eighth century before Christ was
such an one for religion in Judæa. If this was
true of Isaiah's period, what shall be said of the
century that was opened by Jesus Himself,
wherein St. Paul wrote, which St. John closed?
It may be allowed to give the Holy Apostles a
place at the feet of Jesus, and at the same time
to place them above the saints of the generations that were to come. Paul was to Jesus a
slave,—he must ever be to us St. Paul.

When one studies the Epistles he arrives at
two conclusions, and they help to clear up the
situation. It is surely evident that between
the Apostolic writings and those of the after
time, from the Fathers to present-day theologians, there is a gulf fixed. Certain scholars
may question, without profanity, the inclu-
sion of the Book of Esther in Holy Scripture ;

certain others may deny, with less show of reason, any useful function to the Book of Ecclesiastes. Many value the *Imitation* next to their Bible, and more might give this place to the *Pilgrim's Progress*. But no one in his religious senses, however he may be tempted to undervalue some minor books in the canon, or honour above their value some books of the later time, would seriously propose to add À Kempis and Bunyan to the Epistles. It would be an impossible action, equivalent to alternating Mr. Holman Hunt and Mr. Long with Perugino and Sarto. There is a difference between the old masters and the modern which does not need to be put into words, because it is felt by people quite ignorant of art. This is not a depreciation of the moderns: it is an appreciation of the Apostles.

In the same way it must surely strike any one passing from the Gospels into the Epistles, and comparing the words of Jesus with the writings of St. Paul, that the Apostle is less than his Master. Between the Thessalonian and the Philippian Epistles there is of course an immense advance in vision and charity, and throughout every letter there is a profound spiritual genius. St. Paul's devotion to the Person of Christ, his grasp of his Master's teachings, his power in working it up into impressive dogma, his skill in applying Jesus' principles to the conduct of life, his unaffected love for man are so evident, and so exacting, that one shrinks from suggesting that the Apostle as a teacher is less than the greatest. It seems almost profanity to criticise St. Paul, but one may not make him equal to Jesus, without removing Jesus from His judgment seat, and destroying the proportion of Holy Scripture. If one may be pardoned his presumption in hinting at any imperfections in the Apostle of the Gentiles, is not his style at times overwrought by feeling? Are not some of his illustrations forced? Is not his doctrine often rabbinical, rather than Christian? Does not one feel his treatment of certain subjects—say marriage and asceticism—as somewhat wanting in sweetness? One only makes this rebate from the Apostle's excellency in order to magnify the divinity of Jesus' Evangel, which is never local, never narrow, never unintelligible, which is ever calm, convincing, human.

It is a grave question whether, indeed, St.

Paul claimed to be on the same level of authority as Jesus, and can be settled, not by the
production of passages, but rather by reference
to the whole tone of his letters. Was he not
ever the reverent student and faithful expositor
of the mind of Jesus, declared to him by heaven
and by the inner light? Was he not constantly
overcome by the impossibility of entering fully
into its fathomless depths? Did he not at every
turn bring his converts face to face with Jesus
and leave them at His feet? Could one imagine St. Paul declaring that he had added
to the teaching of Jesus, and that without
his Epistles the Gospels would have had little
value? The question comes really to this:
Ought we to read St. Paul in the light of Jesus,
or Jesus in the light of St. Paul? and it is
difficult to see how any one can hesitate in his
reply who believes either in the divinity of Jesus'
person or the divinity of His teaching.

When Jesus finally committed His divine
teaching into the hands of the eleven apostles
in the upper room, it is superfluous to inquire
whether they understood Him. With the possible exception of St. John, none of them had
more than a faint idea of Jesus' Evangel. What

a pathetic spectacle it was—Jesus pouring forth those eternal words that have opened heaven to faith, and been the bread of the soul in all ages, and those honest, dense children of Judaism interrupting with their hopeless questions. Did Jesus suppose that they were entering into His mind or could expound His words? He was under no fond delusion. Why did He place this priceless treasure in those unconscious hands, and charge such men to be His preachers? Because He was going to the Father, and must leave His word in the hands of stewards who were His faithful friends. Because, notwithstanding their slowness of understanding and various imperfections, the eleven were the most spiritual and receptive men of His day and race. Because, although they had then only a very poor grasp of Jesus' Evangel, and were immediately to forsake the Master, they would yet enter into its heart and do greater works with Jesus' words than He had been able to do Himself.

It must be remembered that when Jesus had said His last word on earth and ascended unto the Father, it was not to cease from teaching any more than from working. He was only to depart in the flesh, having given the letter, that He might return by the Holy Ghost to open up the spirit. As a father He placed in the hands of His children the sum of all His wisdom, not expecting them to understand it at first, but charging them to give themselves to study in the good hope that they would enter into it. The Church has been the child, and the long history of doctrine and morals has been the attempt to possess Jesus' words, while all the time He Himself was the Lord of every one that trusted in Him. Her history as the disciple of Jesus has been a progress from the second century unto this present. After the Apostolic days, still bright with the after-glow of Jesus, there was her childhood, simple, poetical, audacious—a time of allegories; her manhood, strenuous, reasonable, comprehensive—a time of doctrines; then will come her maturity, calm, charitable, certain. We have not seen this last period yet, and must remind ourselves at every turn that the Church has not yet compassed the mind of the Master.

Her progress in the understanding of Jesus has been most confused—sometimes disappointing in its arrestments, sometimes amazing in its rapidity. Prophets have suddenly arisen with a quite wonderful insight into Jesus' meaning, and have made a permanent contribution to the knowledge of the Church. They were doubtless wrong somewhere, but somewhere they were right, and their words remain a footnote on the text of Jesus. Afterwards came times when the intelligence of the Church simply went to sleep, and no true strong word was spoken to the world, or her brain grew delirious, and the Church raved to the offence of the world. There have been times of paralysis and times of inspiration, but through both the Church has still been, on the whole, advancing and entering into truth. It may be claimed that we have a more certain and spiritual apprehension of Jesus than our fathers had, for which we deserve no credit: and it may be hoped that our children will know more than we do—of which they may not boast.

It must be frankly acknowledged that the Church, as the teaching body of Christianity, has often been wrong, and the list of exploded errors suggests various reflections. Who would now believe such doctrines as reprobation of human souls by God, the denial of

the divine Fatherhood, and the identity of punishment with vengeance? But one must not
forget or undervalue the discoveries made by
Christian thought and piety. For instance,
the fourth century wrought out a theory of
Jesus' person which may be misused so that it
becomes a stumbling-block to reason instead
of a help to faith, but which stands until this
day the most satisfactory key to a great mystery, and the most complete proof of the unity
of the spiritual universe. The Reformers faced
the problem of the sinner and God, and lodged
in the minds of most thinking men that no
other Mediator had ever existed or was needed
save the Son of Man, and this spiritual fact
can be held apart from all theories of the atonement which come and go with different ages.
The Church is now asking what Jesus expects
His disciples to do for their fellow-men, and no
one doubts that we are being led into the
Divine Will. The service of man has always
lain hid in Jesus' words, but now it has been
made manifest and is taking hold of us like a
revelation. There is no finality in this development, although from time to time the Church
herself has tried to set a bound. Year by year

Jesus' teaching yields new doctrines, new duties, new motives, new hopes, as the soil turned over and exposed to the sun fertilizes dormant seeds and brings them to perfection.

This progress is a convincing evidence of the indwelling Spirit of Jesus, whom the Master promised to send into His disciples' hearts, and whose guidance we unhesitatingly recognise in the Acts of the Apostles. Many persons seem to believe that the operations of Jesus' Spirit closed with the apostolic period, and would not hold that the modern Church is under the same divine influence as the Church of Judæa. But this surely is an untenable, and, if one go into it, an unbelieving position. No doubt the Council of Jerusalem, which had to decide whether Christianity was to be a Jewish sect or a world-wide religion, had a critical duty to discharge, but not more serious than the Council of Nice which affirmed Christ's deity; and if the former Council was justified in saying, ' It seemed good to the Holy Ghost and to us,' the latter had as much right to use the same preface. If the Church at Antioch was moved by the Holy Ghost to send forth Barnabas and Paul on the first foreign mission, surely it was

by the inspiration of the same Spirit that half
a dozen faithful men met in an English town
and sent Carey to India. Why should we
question that the Spirit of Jesus was in the
Council of Trent and the Westminster Assembly? It was disappointing that Trent did not
give relief from the tyranny of the priesthood ;
yet it did reform the discipline of the Roman
Church : that Westminster ignored the evan-
gelisation of the world, yet it conceived a very
majestic idea of God. One does not forget the
blazing mistakes of Church Councils, from that
which ordered the celibacy of the clergy to the
one which declared the infallibility of the pope,
from the Swiss Synod which asserted the inspiration of the vowel points in Hebrew to the
Scottish Assembly which cast out as a heretic
M'Leod Campbell. This does not mean that
the Spirit of Jesus has forsaken His disciples ;
it only means that He is constantly hindered
by His instruments. It is not wonderful that
the Church has erred ; it is wonderful that, in
spite of many a blundering and weakening influence, she has so fully entered into the truth
of Jesus.

THE SOVEREIGNTY OF
CHARACTER

III

THE SOVEREIGNTY OF CHARACTER

Christians with a sense of fitness are not ambitious to claim originality for their Master, and have forgotten themselves when they ground Jesus' position on the brilliancy of His thought. They shrink, as by an instinct, from entering Jesus for competition with other teachers, and have Him so enshrined in the soul that to praise Him seems profanity. When a biographer of Jesus, more distinguished perhaps by his laborious detail than his insight into truth, seriously recommends Jesus to the notice of the world by certificates from Rousseau and Napoleon, or when some light-hearted man of letters embroiders a needy paragraph with a string of names where Jesus is wedged in between Zoroaster and Goethe, the Christian consciousness is aghast. This treatment is not merely bad taste; it is impossible by any canon

D

of thought; it is as if one should compare the sun with electric light, or the colour of Titian with the bloom of the rose. We criticise every other teacher; we have an intuition of Jesus. He is not a subject of study, He is a revelation to the soul—that or nothing. One does not dream of claiming intellectual pre-eminence for Jesus; one is ready, at this point, to make the largest admissions. Why should we bring Him into comparison with Socrates? He does not come within the same category, raising no subtle problems, nor making fine swordplay with words. It is open to debate, indeed, whether Jesus said anything absolutely new, save when He taught the individual to call God Father. Very likely, with the exception of a few *obiter dicta*, you could piece out the Sermon on the Mount from the Old Testament; certainly Plato has a remarkable anticipation of the Cross. Why should we force the battle of parallel columns on the pedantic minority who depreciate Jesus, and put them to the labour of wearisome quotation from the sacred books of the East? Granted, we cry at once, that this saying and the other can be duplicated; for even stout hearts are now beginning to fail at a hint of S'âkyamuni.

We abandon the plain before the heavy artillery lumbers up, without any sense of loss. Originality is not an addition to knowledge; it is only a new arrangement of colour.

Originality in literature is called discovery in science, and the lonely supremacy of Jesus rests not on what He said, but on what He did. Jesus is absolute Master in the sphere of religion, which is a science dealing not with intellectual conceptions, but with spiritual facts. His ideas are not words, they are laws; they are not thoughts, they are forces. He did not suggest, He asserted what He had seen by direct vision. He did not propose, He commanded as one who knew there was no other way. One of His chief discoveries was a new type of character, His greatest achievement its creation. It is now nineteen centuries since He lived on earth, but to-day in every country of the western world there are men differing from their neighbours, as Jesus did from His contemporaries. Jesus was a type by Himself, and they are of the same type. One of course does not mean that the type can be recognised in every Christian, or that it can be seen complete in any, but that if you take a sufficient number of

Jesus' disciples you will discover in their habits of thinking and acting a certain trend of character, which was not known before Jesus came, and apart from His Spirit could not now exist, which also would die out in three generations were His Spirit withdrawn. He presented to the world a solitary ideal, and in innumerable lives He has made it real.

When Jesus began to be a force in human life, there were four existent types on which men formed themselves and which are still in evidence. One is the moral, and has the Jew for its supreme illustration, with his faith in the eternal, and his devotion to the law of righteousness. The next is the intellectual, and was seen to perfection in the Greek, whose restless curiosity searched out the reason of things, and whose æsthetic taste identified beauty and divinity. The third is the political, and stood enthroned at Rome, where a nation was born in the purple and dictated order to the world. And the last is the commercial, and had its forerunner in the Phœnician, who was the first to teach the power of enterprise and the fascination of wealth. Any other man born at the beginning of the first century

could be dropped into his class, but Jesus
defied classification. As He moved among the
synagogues of Galilee, He was an endless perplexity. One could never anticipate Him. One
was in despair to explain Him. Whence is He?
the people whispered with a vague sense of the
problem, for He marked the introduction of a
new form of life. He was not referable to
type: He was the beginning of a time.

Jesus did not repeat the *rôle* of Moses. He
did not forbid His disciples to steal or tell lies;
it would have been a waste of His power to
teach the alphabet of morals. He takes morality
for granted, and carves what Moses has hewn.
His great discourse moves not in the sphere of
duty but in the atmosphere of love. ' It hath
been said, Thou shalt love thy neighbour. . . .
I say unto you, Love your enemies.' His disciples' righteousness must ' exceed the righteousness of the Scribes and Pharisees.' They must
not only do as much as, but ' more than others.'
The legal measure is morality, and the overflow
Christianity. Jesus stands above Judaism, and
He is an alien to Hellenism. Writers without
any sense of proportion have tried to graft
Greek culture on St. Paul because he was born

at Tarsus, and quoted once or twice from Greek poets; but no one has suggested that Jesus owed anything to letters. He wrote no book; He formed no system ; His words were jets of truth, and chose their own forms. The Empire was not within the consciousness of Jesus : His only point of contact with Rome was the Cross. When His following wished to make Him a King, He shuddered and fled as from an insult. As for wealth, it seemed so dangerous that He laid poverty as a condition on His disciples, and Himself knew not where to lay His head. You cannot trace Jesus : you cannot analyse Jesus. His intense spirituality of soul, His simplicity of thought, His continual self-abnegation, and His unaffected humility descended on a worn-out, hopeless world, like dew upon the dry grass.

The Sermon on the Mount has been until lately very much shelved by theologians, but it remains the manifesto of Jesus' religion, and carries in spirit His own irresistible charm—the freshness of new revelation. ' Blessed,' said Jesus, opening His mouth with intention, and no one could have guessed what would follow. The world had its own idea of blessedness. Blessed is the man who is always right. Blessed is the man who is satisfied with himself. Blessed is the man who is strong. Blessed is the man who rules. Blessed is the man who is rich. Blessed is the man who is popular. Blessed is the man who enjoys life. These are the beatitudes of sight and this present world. It comes with a shock and opens a new realm of thought, that not one of these men entered Jesus' mind when He treated of blessedness. 'Blessed,' said Jesus, 'is the man who thinks lowly of himself ; who has passed through great trials ; who gives in and endures ; who longs for perfection ; who carries a tender heart ; who has a passion for holiness ; who sweetens human life ; who dares to be true to conscience.' What a conception of character ! Blessed are the humble, the penitents, the victims, the mystics, the philanthropists, the saints, the mediators, the confessors. For the first time a halo rests on gentleness, patience, kindness, and sanctity, and the eight men of the beatitudes divide the kingdom of God.

Jesus afterwards focussed the new type of character in a lovely illustration which is not always appreciated at its full value, because we deny it perspective. Every reader of the Gospels has marked the sympathy of Jesus with children. How He watched their games! How angry He was with His disciples for belittling them! How He used to warn men, whatever they did, never to hurt a little child! How grateful were children's praises when all others had turned against Him! One is apt to admire the beautiful sentiment, and to forget that children were more to Jesus than helpless, gentle creatures to be loved and protected. They were His chief parable of the kingdom of heaven. As a type of character the kingdom was like unto a little child, and the greatest in the kingdom would be the most child-like. According to Jesus, a well-conditioned child illustrates better than anything else on earth the distinctive features of Christian character. Because he does not assert nor aggrandise himself. Because he has no memory for injuries, and no room in his heart for a grudge. Because he has no previous opinions, and is not ashamed to confess his ignorance. Because he can imagine, and has the key of another world, entering in through the ivory gate and living amid the things unseen and eternal. The new society of Jesus was a magnificent imagination, and he who entered it must lay aside the world standards and ideals of character, and become as a little child.

Jesus was an absolute and unreserved believer in character, and was never weary of insisting that a man's soul was more than his environment, and that he must be judged not by what he held and had, but by what he was and did. Nothing could be easier than to say, ' Lord, Lord,' but that did not count. Jesus' demand was to do the ' will of My Father which is in heaven,' and all of this kind made one family. He only has founded a kingdom on the basis of character; He only has dared to believe that character will be omnipotent. No weapon in Jesus' view would be so winsome, so irresistible, as the beatitudes in action. His disciples were to use no kind of force, neither tradition, nor miracles, nor the sword, nor money. They were to live as He lived, and influence would conquer the world. Jesus elected twelve men—one was a failure—and trained them till they thought with Him, and saw with Him. St. John did not imitate Jesus, he assimilated Jesus. Each disciple became a centre himself, and so the kingdom grows by multiplying and widening circles of influence.

The aggression of Jesus is the propagation of character. 'Ye are the salt of the earth,' 'Ye are the light of the world.' The victory of Jesus is to be the victory of character. 'In the regeneration (Utopia) when the Son of Man shall sit in the throne of His glory, ye also shall sit upon twelve thrones, judging the twelve tribes of Israel.'

When Jesus grounds His religion on character He gives a radiant proof of His sanity and wins at once the suffrages of reasonable men. There is nothing on which we differ so hopelessly as creed, nothing on which we agree so utterly as character. Impanel twelve men of clean conscience and average intelligence and ask them to try some person by his opinions, and they may as well be discharged at once. They will not agree till the Greek Kalends. Ask them to take the standard of conduct, and they will bring in a verdict in five minutes. They have agreed in anticipation. Just as he approximates to the beatitudes they will pronounce the man good; just as he diverges will they declare him less than good. Were any one to insinuate a reference to his opinions, it would be instantly dismissed as an irrelevance, and worse, an immorality, an attempt to confuse the issues of justice. According to the consistent teaching of Jesus a Christian is one of the same likeness as Himself, and nothing will more certainly debauch the religious sense than any shifting of labels, so that one who keeps Jesus' commandments is denied His name, and one in whom there is no resemblance to Jesus receives it on grounds of correct opinion. One cannot imagine our Master requiring the world to accept a disciple on the ground of the man's declaration of faith; He would offer to the world the test of the man's life. When one puts in his faith as evidence he is giving a cheque on a bank beyond reach; when he puts in his character he pays in gold. The reasonableness of Jesus carries everything before it. 'Do men gather grapes of thorns, or figs of thistles? Even so every good tree bringeth forth good fruit, but a corrupt tree bringeth forth evil fruit.' 'Wherefore by their fruits ye shall know them.'

With His appreciation of character Jesus affords us a ground of certitude which can be found nowhere else in religion. This is where Christian ethics have an enormous advantage

over Christian theology. One generation may
build up a doctrine with the most conscientious labour, but it has no guarantee that the
next—equally earnest and intelligent—may not
reverse it, laying the emphasis on other texts,
or influenced by some other spirit. There can
be no finality in theology: this is one of its
glories. Therefore it must ever be an uncer-
tain ground of judgment: this is one of its dis-
abilities. One century a Christian is burned
because he does not believe in the Mass, and in
the next another is executed because he does.
It were patent injustice to bind up salvation
with a fluctuating science; condemnation
might then hinge on the date of a man's birth,
not the attitude of his soul. There are only
two departments in which the human mind can
arrive at certainty: one is pure mathematics,
and the other is pure ethics. The whole must
be greater than its part, not only in this world
but in every other where the same rational
order prevails, and there can be no place within the moral order where the man of the beatitudes will not be judged perfect. At no time
and in no circumstances can he be condemned
or depreciated. Yesterday, to-day and for ever

he is the bright excellency of manhood. Again, without effort and without argument, Jesus carries conviction to reason and conscience. 'Whosoever heareth these sayings of Mine, and doeth them, I will liken him unto a wise man, which built his house upon a rock.'

It would, however, be a shallow inference that the premium Jesus set on character meant a discount on faith, or that Jesus has originated that exasperating contrast between creed and life. If Jesus, magnifying character, said in one discourse, 'Be ye therefore perfect even as your Father which is in heaven is perfect,' He made it plain in another how character is formed: 'Except ye eat the flesh of the Son of Man and drink His blood, ye have no life in you.' He insisted on being, and also on believing, and in His mind they fell into order. Faith in Him was the process, and character was the product, and Jesus with His supreme reasonableness taught that the finished product and not the varying process should be the material of judgment. It is vain to expatiate on the ingenuity of the machinery if the sample of corn be badly milled; and if it be well done the criticism on the machinery may be spared.

If any one is so fortunate as to hold in his heart and in its fulness the Catholic faith concerning Jesus, his richly developed character will be the unanswerable vindication of his creed. If one, less fortunate, should miss that full vision of Jesus, which is the inheritance of the saints, then it will be unnecessary to criticise his creed, since a frost-bitten and poverty-stricken character will be its swift condemnation. 'He that abideth in Me and I in him, the same bringeth forth much fruit' is Jesus' reconciliation of creed and character.

One cannot yield to the force of Jesus' teaching on character without facing its last application and asking, Will the final Assize be held on faith or character? As a matter of fact, the best public mind under all religions has judged by character, and has done so with a keen sense of justice and a conviction of paramount authority. When the individual has to form an estimate of his neighbour in critical circumstances he ignores his opinions and weighs his virtues. No one, for instance, would leave his wife and children to the care of a trustee because he happened to be a Trinitarian, but only because his friend was a true man before God. It is a working principle of life that judgment goes by character, and if in the end it should go by faith it might be in keeping with some higher justice we know not here; but it would cover our moral sense with confusion and add another to the unintentional wrongs men have endured, in this world, at their fellows' hands. It were useless to argue about a matter of which we know nothing and where speculation is vain. We must simply accept the words of Jesus, and it is an unspeakable relief to find our Master crowning His teaching on character with the scene of the Last Judgment. The prophecy of conscience will not be put to shame, nor the continuity of this life be broken. When the parabolic form is reduced and the accidental details laid aside, it remains that the Book of Judgment is the Sermon on the Mount, and that each soul is tried by its likeness to the Judge Himself. Jesus has prepared the world for a startling surprise, but it will not be the contradiction of our present moral experience: it will be the revelation of our present hidden character.

AGELESS LIFE

IV

AGELESS LIFE

Jesus reigns supreme among teachers not only by the perfection of His character but also by the grandeur of His subject. A prophet has many things to say to his generation ; one only is his message. Jesus treated every idea of the first order in the sphere of Religion; His burden was Life. He did not set Himself to teach men how to organise the state, nor how to analyse their minds, nor how to discharge elementary duties, nor how to form a science of Theology. This was not because Jesus despised these departments, it was because He proposed to dominate them. He would not localise Himself in one because He would inspire all. Behind the state is the individual, behind the individual is the soul, and the one question of the soul is life. The soul is the organ, and life the function ; and although exact scholars may be horrified, the translators of our Bible had hold of the facts of the case when they used a certain word generously, rendering it in one verse 'life' and in the next 'soul.' Ethical life implies the soul, and a dead soul is a contradiction in terms. The chief necessity of man is life, and when Jesus opened its spring He fertilised human nature to its farthest border. He was not a Politician, but the Democracy is His creation; He was not a Philosopher, but He has given us the modern metaphysic; He was not a Moralist, but He has inspired the coming ethic; He was not a Theologian, but the creeds are built out of His teaching. He revived the body of humanity by the regeneration of the individual. Before Jesus, life was a wistful longing: it was also a hopeless mystery. With the thinkers of one nation it was a speculation, as in the *Phædo;* with the saints of another it was a vision, as in the sixteenth Psalm. Jesus brought life to light and declared the doctrine of immortality. History acknowledges Him as the first and last authority on the biology of the soul, and experience has proved Him to be the only medium of life. Life was the gift

Jesus carried in His hand; as He said, in His magnificent way, ' I am come that they might have life, and that they might have it more abundantly.'

An instinct is any part of our spiritual capital which has not been contributed by education or revelation, and our two chief instincts are God and immortality. The hope of the future life has always nestled in the heart of the race, and found wings upon occasion. When savages bury his weapons and utensils with the dead man in order that he may start with a full equipment, they believe that he is somewhere ; and when the Athenians went out to Eleusis twice a year, in March as the life of the year springs, and in September as it fades, and held a solemn function, it was not only that they might live happily, but, as Cicero puts it, ' might die with a fairer hope.' The Eleusinian mysteries must have been a great support to the pious of the day, and served the purpose of a conference for the deepening of spiritual life. This instinct dies down to the root in the winter of Agnosticism, but it never loses its vitality. Clever people point out that no one can demonstrate immortality,—which goes without saying ; and high-minded people condemn the desire for continued individuality as a subtle form of selfishness,—which is very superior. There may be an insignificant minority who would be content that their life should be flung back like a cupful of water into the stream from which it was taken. But to the race the destruction of this hope would be irreparable, since it is laden with a wealth of compensation and reparation. Mourners are content because those 'loved long since' are only 'lost awhile.' St. Stephen, cut off in his youth, does not complain, because he sees Jesus standing at God's right hand. The scholar gathers his apparatus for unending work.

> 'What's time? Leave Now for dogs and apes
> Man has Forever.'

Arthur, betrayed and beaten, does not despair :

> 'My God, Thou hast forgotten me in my death :'
> 'Nay, God my Christ, I pass, but shall not die.'

This sublime instinct Jesus found and did not belittle. He confirmed it with His sanction and built on it His doctrine of Ageless Life.

It was not Jesus' function to add to our nature; it was His to glorify it, and in His hands the instinct of immortality was raised to its highest power. Jesus began with a tacit distinction between existence and life which gives a characteristic lift and splendour to His words. Existence is physical, and is dependent on the energy that works in matter. Life is spiritual, and is dependent on the energy that works in mind. One comes upon a person that has not one point of contact with the thought-world : he eats, digests, moves,—we say he exists. One comes on another full of ideas, plans, dreams, ambitions,—we say he is alive. It is the approximate statement of a fact in human history. When the former dies we are not astonished, because it had never struck us that he was alive. When the latter dies we are shocked, the disappearance of that radiant man is a catastrophe. Jesus recognised similar conditions in the spiritual world—existence, which meant an inert and unconscious soul, and life, which meant a soul receptive and active. Mere existence He called death, and used to startle men into thinking with paradoxes : 'Let the dead bury their dead;' 'Verily, verily, I say unto you, the hour is coming and now is when the dead shall hear the voice of the Son of God, and they that hear shall live.' Whether Jesus believed in the continued existence of this lowest grade in the human kingdom can hardly be disputed when in this parable we read that a soul eaten up by selfishness like Dives, and a soul purified by trial like Lazarus, both reappeared in another world. Jesus assumed existence for all, but existence on this low plane of death was not worth His consideration. Jesus was not an authority on existence; His field was life. He did not labour the barren theory of conscious immortality apart from the condition of the soul: but He transforms immortality into Life by charging immortality with an ethical content and making it to consist in the knowledge of God: ' This is Life Eternal, that they might know Thee the only true God, and Jesus Christ whom Thou hast sent.'

When Jesus invested Life with its new meaning He glorified the idea, but He was embarrassed with the word. Words were polarized before Jesus adopted them, and they were apt to retain their acquired properties in His Kingdom. Nothing could have done full justice to the ideas of Jesus save a new language, and, as that was impossible, Jesus and His disciples were often at cross purposes. With Him Life was something eternal and absolute; with them,

something limited and temporary. Life suggested nothing to them at first, except the vitality of the body ; death, nothing except its dissolution. Jesus, on His part, never used Life and
Death in a physical sense with emphasis, unless
when He spoke of laying down His own Life,
and no one knows what was hidden in that mystery. 'I have power to lay it down, and I have
power to take it again.' He reserved the words
for their highest use, and ignored the popular
reading. 'Our friend Lazarus,' He said, with
careful choice of terms, 'sleepeth ; but I go,
that I may awake him out of sleep.' Lazarus,
the brother of Mary, and the friend of Jesus,
could not be dead. It was a moral impossibility. The Jews who saw Jesus at Lazarus'
tomb and played the informer to the Pharisees
were dead. It was a moral necessity. When
the misunderstanding was hopeless Jesus had to
condescend. 'Lazarus,' if I must speak in your
tongue, 'is dead.' Physical death Jesus refused
to recognise ; it was an incident in the history of
Life. Death was a calamity of the soul, and a
living soul was invulnerable. 'I am the Resurrection and the Life : he that believeth in Me,
though he were dead, yet shall he live : and

whosoever liveth, and believeth in Me, shall never die.' It was a brave struggle for reality, and liberated the first disciples from the bondage of the physical; but the atmosphere is too rare for His modern disciples, who, for the most part, speak exactly as if they were Pagans in the Street of Tombs at Athens, instead of Christians who had sat at Jesus' feet.

Jesus had to contend with a more inexcusable misuse which binds up the life of a man, not with his body, but with his material environment. According to this squalid definition, Life is made up of circumstances; if they are pleasant, the man has an easy life; if they are adverse, he has a hard life. Life is stated in terms of food and raiment, and goods and houses. Against this degradation of life Jesus lifted up His voice in a protest which admits of no answer. He was never weary of reminding His disciples that such things could not constitute Life, and were, indeed, so unworthy as to be beneath care. 'A man's life consisteth not in the abundance of the things which he possesseth.' 'Take no thought for your life, what ye shall eat, or what ye shall drink; nor yet for your body, what ye shall put on. Is not the life more than meat, and the body than raiment?' 'Labour not for the meat which perisheth, but for that meat which endureth unto everlasting life, which the Son of Man shall give unto you.' Certainly this indifference to circumstances was not due to any want of sympathy with the labouring and heavy laden—witness His parables, or to the favoured experiences of His own life—witness His poverty. But Jesus was anxious to lift Life above the tyranny of circumstances and convince His followers that one could live like God Himself, although he had a whole world arrayed against him and left nothing behind him except a peasant's garment. And Jesus was jealous lest they should confound the rough scaffolding of circumstances, within which the building was slowly rising, with the Temple of Life itself.

Jesus has bequeathed to the world a monograph on life (St. John vi.), and its basal idea is Unity. Spiritual Life is not a series of isolated springs, but an ocean laving every shore. It is one and has its source in God, as Truth and Righteousness and Love are one and stand in God. When one thinks of Life in man as one thing, and Life in God as another, he has lost the key to the science of Life. Nothing deserves the name of Life in us that cannot be affirmed of God. Life in the soul is the tide of the Divine ocean flowing as it has opportunity through the narrow channels of human nature. Everything else is only a colourable imitation of Life, and a mode of existence. Life is in its origin Heavenly, and cometh down. One must be 'born from above' if he is to enter into Life. Jesus casts His contrast between physical and spiritual Life into a felicitous figure. 'Your fathers did eat manna in the wilderness, and are dead. This is the bread which cometh down from Heaven, that a man may eat thereof, and not die.' Life is first in God who is in Heaven, inaccessible, and next in Jesus who is incarnate, and finally in any man who is in fellowship with Jesus. 'As the living Father hath sent Me, and I live by the Father; so he that eateth Me, even he shall live by Me.' This is Jesus' theory of Life.

The second idea which underlies this discourse is Community. Jesus and His disciples share the same Life. He is the 'Bread of

Life,' and they ' eat.' Jesus with this startling
image flashes a description of Life and answers
the question, ever in the background of one's
mind, ' What is Life?' It is fellowship with
the Spirit of Jesus, something that cannot be
estimated by the beating of the pulse, or the
inventory of a man's possessions, that must be
tested by conscience and the intangible scales
of the Kingdom of Heaven. It will lie in a
certain mind, in a certain ruling motive, in a
certain trend of character, in a certain obedience of will, in a certain passion for goodness,
the same as that of Jesus. Or, as Jesus put it
in a passage misunderstood too often by Jews
and Gentiles, yet simple enough when read according to the mode of Jesus' thinking: ' Whoso
eateth My flesh, and drinketh My blood, hath
eternal life.' This is Jesus' practice of Life.

The third idea which inspires the deliverance
of Jesus is Eternity. Again and again, with
heartening reiteration, Jesus pronounces Life
' everlasting,' and Jesus' expression is evidently
shaped by a contrast. It is His appreciation of
Life ; it is His depreciation of its travesty.
There is, He means, what may by concession
be called life, which consists in health, and riches,

and ease, and pleasure. This is life centred, and imprisoned, and satisfied in this present age. Its environment is local and temporary, and when it is shattered this life must perish, because it has no roots elsewhere. With its age it vanishes. He that findeth this life shall lose it. Life, as Jesus understood it, consisting of Love and Sacrifice, does not belong to any age because it is the inhabitant of all. Its roots are struck into the unchanging and eternal. It has already a spiritual environment, and when this present state of things is removed Life will rise to its full height and find itself at home. This is Life which cannot be lost. Life to-day, it would have been life when the Pyramids were new, it will be Life when the earth is an ice-cold ball. Life is contemporaneous with all the centuries, it anticipates and closes them. 'Time is a parenthesis in eternity,' says a fine old classic. When an earth-born man is baptized into the Spirit of Jesus the brackets are removed and he begins to live in the ageless state. 'He that believeth on Me hath ageless Life.' This is Jesus' prophecy of life.

Life with Jesus was a condition of the soul

disentangled from any physical mode of existence, and with this profound conception before
His mind, He did not need the classical arguments for immortality. One would be surprised if Jesus proved the future life from the
analogies of nature or the law of continuity.
One would be as much surprised if He described
its circumstances even in the sublime poetry of
St. John or followed the soul in its experiences
as in the *Book of the Dead*. For one moment
we do wonder why Jesus, who, alone of all men
in this world, had been within the veil, did not
describe at length the details of the unseen
state; in the next we understand such an
apocalypse would have been alien to Jesus.
Life before His eyes was not divided into sec-
tions, each depending for its character on local
colouring. Life here and there—everywhere—
in its essence and intention, must be the same
—conformity to the Divine Will—an inward
peace and joy. As a man lived here in this
age, he would live in all the ages; carrying
Heaven within Him rather than going into
Heaven. The Life of the soul could not be
affected by the death of the body. Jesus
would have considered the question, 'Shall I

live after death?' beside the mark. He would have asked, 'Have you life now?' for Life is ageless.

If one should insist on proof that Life is ageless, then Jesus was content to offer Himself. Life hinges on this word of Jesus, 'Because I live, ye shall live also.' Suppose Jesus was the victim of a fond delusion when He ignored the death of the body and preached the ageless life of the soul and insisted on the unseen, then He is dead.

> 'And on His grave with shining eyes
> The Syrian stars look down.'

Suppose He knew, when He declared Life the supreme fact of human experience, and death the escape of the butterfly from the chrysalis and the world a passing show, then Jesus is alive evermore. How can one be certain that Jesus is with God? It is a question of the last importance. There are four lines of proof. The first is to lead reliable evidence that Jesus rose from Joseph's tomb—this is for a lawyer. The second is historical—the existence of the Christian Church—this is for a scholar. The third is mystical—the experience of Christians—this is for a saint. The fourth is ethical—the nature of Jesus' life—this is for every one. The last is the most akin to the mind of Jesus, who was accustomed to insist on the self-evidencing power of His life. He is alive because He could not die. 'I am the Resurrection and the Life.'

It is impossible to appreciate a picture with your face at the canvas; but even His blind generation were arrested by Jesus. There was a note in His words that caught their ear, the echo of Divine authority; there was an air about Him, the manner of a larger world. No man could convince Him of sin, none confound Him. He was ever beyond criticism. He ever compelled admiration in honest men. 'Thou art the Christ,' said a Jewish peasant with instinctive conviction, 'the Son of the Living God.' Centuries have only confirmed this spontaneous tribute to Jesus' life. No one has yet discovered the word Jesus ought not to have said, none suggested the better word He might have said. No action of His has shocked our moral sense; none has fallen short of the ideal. He is full of surprises, but they are all the surprises of perfection. You are never amazed, one day

F

by His greatness, the next by His littleness. You are ever amazed that He is incomparably better than you could have expected. He is tender without being weak, strong without being coarse, lowly without being servile. He has conviction without intolerance, enthusiasm without fanaticism, holiness without Pharisaism, passion without prejudice. This Man alone never made a false step, never struck a jarring note. His life alone moved on those high levels where local limitations are transcended and the absolute Law of Moral Beauty prevails. It was life at its highest. Jesus was the supreme Artist in Life, and had a right to say, ' I am the Life.'

Was this Life something that could be quenched by death or that death could touch? Granted that they scourged and crucified Jesus' body, that it died and was buried. Could Jesus who gave the Sermon on the Mount and the discourse of the upper room, who satisfied St. John and loosed St. Mary Magdalene from her sin, and who remains the unapproachable ideal of perfection, be annihilated by a few nails and the thrust of a Roman spear? If the lowest form of energy, however it may be transformed

or degraded, be still conserved in some shape
and place, can any one believe that the Author
of Life in this world was extinguished on a
Roman cross? The certainty of Jesus' Resurrection does not rest in the last issue on His
isolated appearances during the forty days; it
rests on His Life for thirty-three years. His
Life was beyond the reach of death; it was
Ageless Life.

Jesus' Life impressed His generation as unparalleled and inexplicable, a Life with inscru-
table motives and incalculable principles. What
was its explanation according to any known
standard? Jesus was accustomed frankly to
admit that it had none; that it was an enigma
from the earthly standpoint. But He pleaded
that it was supreme and reasonable from the
Heavenly standpoint. It was foreign here; it
was natural elsewhere. He did the works He
had seen His Father do, He said the words He
had received of His Father, He fulfilled the
will of His Father. There was a sphere where
His Life was the rule, where His dialect was
the language of the country and His was the
habit of living. His unlikeness to this world
implies His likeness to another world. One

evening you find among the reeds of your lake an unknown bird, whose broad breast and powerful pinions are not meant for this inland scene. It is resting midway between two oceans, and by to-morrow will have gone. Does not that bird prove the ocean it left, does it not prove the ocean whither it has flown? ' Jesus, knowing . . . that He was come from God and went to God,' is the Revelation and Confirmation of Ageless Life.

SIN AN ACT OF SELF-WILL

V

SIN AN ACT OF SELF-WILL

Sin is the ghost which haunts Literature, a shadow on human life, which no one admits he has seen, and which an hour afterwards asserts itself. Define sin with anything like accuracy, and it will be denied; be silent as if you had not heard of sin, and it will be confessed. Literature oscillates between extremes, and affords an instructive contradiction. As the record of human experience it must chronicle sin; as the solace of the individual, it makes a brave effort to ignore sin. You hear the moan of this calamity through all the work of Sophocles, but Aristophanes persuades you that this is the gayest of worlds, and both voices were heard in the same theatre beneath the shadow of enthroned Wisdom. Juvenal's mordant satire lays bare the ulcerous Roman life, but Catullus flings a wreath of roses over it, and they were both poets of the classical age. A French novelist, with an unholy mastery of his craft, steeps us in the horrors of a decadent society. A French critic, with the airiest grace, exclaims: 'Sin, I have abolished it.' Our own poet of unbelief has dared to write, revealing the thoughts of many hearts:—

> ' Alas, Lord ! surely Thou art great and fair,
>   But, lo ! her wonderfully woven hair ;
>   And Thou didst heal us with Thy piteous kiss ;
>   But see now, Lord, her mouth is lovelier.'

Yet he also allows the secret to ooze out—

> ' The brief, bitter bliss one has for a great sin.'

Literature has confessed this mysterious presence twice over, in the hopeless sadness of the austere school which acknowledges it, in the nervous anxiety of the lighter school which scoffs at it.

Philosophy has been, for the most part, distinguished by its strenuous treatment of the moral problem, but has been visibly hampered by circumstances, being in the position of a court which cannot go into the whole case. Sin may be only a defect, then philosophy can cope with the position ; but it is at least possible that sin may be a collision with the will of God, then philosophy can afford no help. Spiritual affairs are beyond its jurisdiction ; they belong to the department of Religion. Within the range of philosophy the Race has not gone astray—it has simply not arrived : humanity is not diseased— it is only poorly developed. This deliverance is not the fault, it is the misfortune of morals ; but it must always seem shallow and unworthy to serious minds. It creates the demand for Religion. If your chest be narrow, you go to a gymnast ; if it be diseased, you go to a physician. It is easy to add three inches to the chest cavity ; it is less easy to kill the bacilli in the lungs. There can indeed be no real competition between Philosophy and Religion, for the former cannot go beyond hygiene, and the latter must begin at least with therapeutics.

'The cardinal question is that of sin,' says Amiel, with his fine ethical insight ; and if it be an essential condition in every religion that it deal with sin, then, excluding Judaism as a provisional and prophetic faith, there are only two religions. One is Christianity, and the other is Buddhism, and the disciples of Jesus need not fear a comparison. When Jesus and the founder of Buddhism address themselves to the problem of evil, the 'Light of Asia' is simply a foil to our

Master. Buddha identified evil with the material influences of the body, as if a disembodied spirit could not be proud and envious; Jesus traced evil to the will, and ignored the body. Buddha proposes to train the soul by a life of meditation, as if inaction could be the nursery of character; Jesus insists on action, the most unremitting and intense. Finally, the great Eastern sage held out the hope of escape from individual existence, as if that were the last reward for the tried soul; our Master promised perfection in the kingdom of heaven. Both systems recognise the supreme need of the Race, which is a favourable omen: they differ in the means of its relief. Buddhism amounts to the destruction of the disease, and the extinction of the patient. Christianity compasses the destruction of the disease, and the salvation of the soul. Tried by the severest test of a Religion, Jesus alone out of all masters remains: He saves ' His people from their sins.'

If Jesus had never said one word, yet had He done more than all writers on sin, for His life was its everlasting exposure. As the undriven snow puts to shame the whitest garment, so was Jesus a new standard of holiness to His society, and as the lightning plays round the steel rod, so did the diffused wickedness of His time concentrate on His head. Pharisees in a heat of pseudo-morality became self-conscious, and slunk from His presence, Who could not look at them, and an honest man of vast self-conceit beheld in a sudden flash the moral glory of Jesus, and besought Him to depart. Twice Jesus was carried beyond Himself by anger—once when St. Peter tempted Him to selfishness, and He identified the amazed apostle with Satan; once when the hyprocisy of the Pharisees came to a head, and His indignation burst forth in the invective of history. He shudders visibly in the Gospels before the loathsome leprosy of sin, while His compassions lighten on the sinner, and in the same Gospels we see the hatred of the world culminate in the Cross, because Jesus did the works of God. The personality of Jesus called the principle of evil into full action, and sin was an open secret before His eyes.

The conventional history of sin has three chapters—origin, nature, treatment. It is characteristic of Jesus that He has only two: He omits genesis and proceeds to diagnosis. It is for an instant a disappointment, and in the next a relief: it remains forever a lesson.

Among all the problems upon which the human intellect has tried its teeth, the origin of evil is the most useless and hopeless, the most fascinating and maddening.   Eastern religions have played the fool with it, Christian theology has laboured it without conspicuous success.   Science has recently been dallying with it.   It is a kind of whirlpool which sucks in the most subtle intellects, and reduces them to confusion. Jesus did not once approach the subject : He alone had the courage to leave it in shadow. As a consequence He has offered another pledge of His reasonableness, and removed a stumbling-block from the doctrine of sin.   Jesus' silence did not arise from indifference to the law of heredity, for He traced the blind hostility of the Pharisees to the bigotry of their fathers, and saw in the sin of His crucifixion the legitimate outcome of ages of fanaticism.   But He foresaw how the moral sense might be perverted by wild applications of the law, as when His disciples asked, ' Who did sin, this man or his parents, that he was born blind ? '   Jesus would, no doubt, know the Rabbinical theory of Adam, although He escaped St. Paul's doubtful advantage, and had not been educated in the

schools; but one feels by an instinct that
Jesus' missing discourse on the 'Federal Relationship' would not fit in well between the
Sermon on the Mount and the Farewell of the
Last Supper. Jesus must have been taught
the story of the Fall, and in after years He en-
dorsed its teaching. He clothed that lovely
idyll with a modern dress, and sent it out as
the Parable of the Prodigal Son. It is always
a startling transition from the theologians to
Jesus, and it gives one pause that the supreme
Teacher of religion did not deliver Himself on
original sin. But it is a fact, and Jesus had
His reasons.

For one thing, any insistence on heredity
would have depreciated responsibility, and
Jesus held every man to his own sin. Science
and theology have joined hands in magnifying
heredity and lowering individuality, till a man
comes to be little more than the resultant of
certain forces, a projectile shot forth from the
past, and describing a calculated course. Jesus
made a brave stand for each man as the pos-
sessor of will-power, and master of his life. He
sadly admitted that a human will might be
weakened by evil habits of thought? He de-

clared gladly that the Divine Grace reinforced the halting will : but, with every qualification, decision still rested in the last issue with the man. 'If Thou wilt, Thou canst make me clean,' as if his cure hinged on the Divine Will. Of course, I am willing, said Jesus, and referred the man back to his inalienable human rights. Jesus never diverged into metaphysics, even to reconcile the freedom of the human will with the sovereignty of the Divine. His function was not academic debate, it was the solution of an actual situation. Logically, men might be puppets ; consciously, they were self-determinating, and Jesus said with emphasis, 'Wilt thou ?'

Jesus had another interest in isolating the individual and declining to comprehend him in the race—He compelled his attention. Nothing could have afforded the Pharisees more satisfaction than a discussion on sin. Nothing was more uncomfortable than an examination into their particular sins. A million needle points pressed together make a smooth substance, but one is intolerable. Jesus touched the conscience as with a needle prick, for which He received homage from honest men, and the cross from the dishonest. Before and since Jesus' day people have been invited to hold an inquest on the sin of Adam, and have discharged this function with keen intellectual interest. It was Jesus who made sin of even date, and invited every hearer to see the tragedy of Eden in his own experience.

If one be still disappointed with the marked silence of Jesus on the genesis of sin, let him find his compensation in Jesus' final analysis of sin. Our Master was not accustomed to lay down a definition, and make it a catchword, or to propose a subject and expound it to exhaustion. He does not equip us with a theory to be associated with His name. His method was worthy of Himself, who alone could say, 'Verily, verily,' and was becoming to spiritual truth, which is above theories. It was not the brilliant play of artificial light on a selected object; it was the rising of the sun on the whole sum of things, a gradual, silent, irresistible illumination before which one saw the wreaths of mist lift, and the recesses of the valleys laid open. While Jesus is teaching by allusions to sin, by revelations of the state of holiness, by the clinical treatment of sinners, by incidental glimpses of His own experience in temptation, a complete and full-rounded idea of sin grows before the mind. His disciples hold it, for the most part, in unconsciousness; as soon as they identify it, Jesus' idea is verified.

Two teachers had attempted the diagnosis of sin before Jesus, and Jesus included their conclusions. Moses had wrought into the warp and woof of Jewish conscience the conviction that sin was a crime against the Eternal, and the Psalmists had invested this view with singular pathos. It mattered not what wrong a man did; it was in the last issue the heart of God he touched. And God only could loose him from the intolerable burden of guilt. Sin was not only the transgression of a law written on the conscience, it was a personal offence against the Divine love. Jewish penitence therefore was very tender and humble. 'Against Thee, Thee only have I sinned.' Jesus, in his Monograph on sin, incorporates this discovery when He makes the prodigal say, 'Father, I have sinned against heaven and in Thy sight,' when He teaches to pray, 'Forgive us our trespasses as we forgive them that trespass against us.' Jesus took for granted that sin was a crime.

Plato made the next contribution to the science of sin. He approached the subject from the intellectual side, and laid it down, with great force, that if we knew more we should sin less; and if we knew all we should not sin at all. This view has been discredited by the reduction of knowledge to culture, when it is at once contradicted by history, for the Renaissance, say in Italy, was a period of monstrous iniquity. Read vision for knowledge, and this view verifies itself, for if our human soul saw with clear eye the loathsome shape of moral deformity and the fair proportions of moral beauty it would not be possible to sin. Jesus lends His sanction to Plato when the prodigal comes to himself, and, his delirium over, compares the far country, in its shame and poverty, with his father's home where the servants have enough and to spare. When Jesus insists 'Repent,' He makes the same plea, for repentance is awaking to fact. It is a change of mind. Jesus also believed that sin was a mistake.

Where Jesus went beyond every other teacher was not in the diagnosis of sin: it was in its analysis. He was not the first to discover its

G

symptoms or forms, but He alone has gone to the bottom of things and detected the principle of sin. Wherein does sin consist? is the question to which one must come in the end. Jesus has answered it by tracing down the varied fibrous growth of sins to its one root, and so, while there are many authorities on sins, there is only one on Sin. As when one sings, according to a recent beautiful experiment, on a mass of confused colours, and they arrange themselves into mystical forms of flower or shell, so Jesus breathes on life and the phantasmagoria of sin changes into one plant, with root, and branches, and leaves, and fruit, all organised and consistent. Tried by final tests, and reduced to its essential elements, sin is the preference of self to God, and the assertion of the human will against the will of God. With Jesus, from first to last, sin is selfishness.

It is the achievement of modern science to discover the unity of the physical world. It is one of the contributions of Jesus to reveal the unity of the spiritual world. Before His eyes it was not a scene of chance or confusion, but an orderly system standing in the 'will of God.' This was Jesus' formula for the law of the soul,

which is the principle of thought—for the law
of life, which is the principle of conduct. If
any one did the 'will of God,' he was in harmony with the spiritual universe; if he did his
'own will' he was out of joint. Consciously
and unconsciously each intelligent being made
a choice at every turn, either fulfilling or out-
raging the higher law of his nature, either
entering into or refusing fellowship with God.
Sin is not merely a mistake or a misfit; it is a
deliberate mischoice. It is moral chaos.

Jesus' absolute consistency in His idea of sin
appears both in the standard of holiness to which
He ever appealed and in His fierce resistance
of certain temptations. 'Which of you con-
vinceth Me of sin?' demanded Jesus in one of
His sharpest passages with the Pharisees, and
it was a bolder challenge than we are apt to
imagine. Had Jesus not been able to refer to
some law above the opinions and customs of
any age, a law beyond the tampering of men,—
and yet repeated within every man's soul,—He
had been cast in that bold appeal. He had
violated a local and national order at every
turn, and incurred misunderstanding and cen-
sure. Had he responded to a higher order

which is over all, and which a Pharisee, as much as Himself, was bound to obey? If it could be shown that He was guided by private ends, and that His life was an organized selfishness, then He must be condemned, and the Amen of every honest man would seal the sentence. But if His life was singular because it was not selfish and did not conform to this world, then He must be acquitted. Jesus was jealous on this point, and evidently watched Himself closely, from His repeated assertions of obedience to the Divine will. 'Neither came I of Myself, but He sent Me.' 'I seek not Mine own glory.' 'My meat is to do the will of Him that sent Me.' 'I can of Myself do nothing; as I hear, I judge; and My judgment is just, because I seek not Mine own will, but the will of the Father which hath sent Me.'

Jesus' passionate devotion to the Divine will and His crucifixion of self-will in its most refined forms can be clearly read in the fire of His temptations. From the wilderness to the garden Jesus seems to have been assailed by one trial expressly suited to His noble ends and unstained soul. He was not tempted to do His own work or to refuse the work of God; such temptations

could never have once touched the Servant of
God.   But it was suggested to Jesus that He
might fulfil His calling as the Messiah with far
surer and quicker success if He did not die on
the cross.   Be an imperial Messiah, was in substance the temptation which arose before Jesus
at the beginning of His public life, and which
He described in such vivid imagery to His
disciples.   He resisted it, because this kind of
Messiah was not the will of God.   He accepted
the cross because it was the will of God.   There
are signs that Jesus at one period had a Messi-
anic idea which did not embrace the Cross.
We detect the inward strain ere Jesus' victory
over self-will was complete.   He set His face
'stedfastly' to go to Jerusalem.   He resented
the suggestion of St. Peter with a sudden fierce-
ness.   He was troubled in prospect of the cross.
He was oppressed for a time in the upper room.
Beneath the olive trees of the garden He had
His last encounter with evil, and only when
He said, 'Nevertheless, not My will, but Thine
be done' was the sinlessness of Jesus established.

Jesus cast His whole doctrine of sin into the
Drama of the Prodigal Son, and commands our

adherence by its absolute fidelity to life. The parable moves between the two poles of ideal and real human life—home, where the sons of God live in moral harmony with their Father, which is liberty,—and exile, where they live in riotous disobedience, which is licence. He fixes on His representative sinner, and traces his career with great care and various subtle touches. His father does not compel him to stay at home :—he has free will. The son claims his portion :—he has individuality. He flings himself out of his father's house :—he makes a mischoice. He plays the fool in the far country :—this is the fulfilling of his bent. He is sent out to feed swine :—this is the punishment of sin. He awakes to a bitter contrast :—this is repentance. He returns to obedience :—this is salvation. Salvation is the restoration of spiritual order—the close of a bitter experience. It is the return of the race from its 'Wander Year.'

Jesus rooted all sin in selfishness, but He distinguished two classes of sinners and their punishment. There was the Pharisee, who re-sisted God because he was wilfully blind and filled with pride. There was the Publican, who

forsook God because he was led astray by
wandering desires and evil habits. Sin, in each
case, wrought its own punishment. For the
Pharisee it was paralysis, so that he could not
enter the kingdom; for the Publican it was
suffering, so that he must cut off the right arm
and pluck out the right eye to obtain the kingdom. Heaven, according to Jesus, was to be
with God in our Father's house; hell was to
be away from God, in the far country. Each
man carried his heaven in his heart—'the kingdom is within you'; or his hell in a gnawing
remorse and heat of lust, 'where their worm
dieth not, and the fire is not quenched.'

It is reasonable to expect that Jesus' idea of
salvation will correspond with His idea of sin,
as lock and key, or disease and medicine, and
one is not disappointed. According to Jesus,
the selfish man was lost; the unselfish was
saved, and so He was ever impressing on His
disciples that they must not strive, but serve.
He Himself had come to serve, and He declared
that His sacrifice of Himself would be the redemption of the world. This is Jesus' explanation of the virtue of His death. It was an act
of utter devotion to the will of God, and a

power of emancipation in the hearts of His disciples. As they entered into His Spirit they would be loosened from bondage and escape into liberty. They would be no longer the slaves of sin, for the Son had made them free. Jesus proposed to ransom the race, not by paying a price to the devil or to God, but by loosening the grip of sin on the heart and reinforcing the will. The service of His life and the sacrifice of His death would infuse a new spirit into humanity, and be its regeneration. 'The Son of Man came not to be ministered unto, but to minister, and to give His life a ransom for many.' Within this one pregnant sentence Jesus states His doctrine of sin and salvation, and it offers three pledges of reality. It reduces the different forms of sin to a unity by tracing them all to self-will. It shows the ethical connection between the sin of man and the death of Jesus. And it can be verified in the experience of the saint, which is the story of a long struggle before his will becomes 'the Will of God.'

THE CULTURE OF THE CROSS

VI

THE CULTURE OF THE CROSS

It has been said, with a superb negligence of
Judaism, that Jesus discovered the individual;
it would be nearer the truth to affirm that Jesus
cultivated the individual. Hebrew religion had
endowed each man with the right to say " I," by
inspiring every man with the faith to say God,
and Jesus raised individuality to its highest
power by a regulated process of sanctification.
Nothing is more characteristic of Jesus' method
than His indifference to the many—His devotion to the single soul. His attitude to the
public, and His attitude to a private person
were a contrast and a contradiction. If His work
was likely to cause a sensation, Jesus charged
His disciples to let no man know it: if the
people got wind of Him, He fled to solitary
places: if they found Him, as soon as might be,
He escaped. But He used to take young men

home with Him, who wished to ask questions:
He would spend all night with a perplexed
scholar: He gave an afternoon to a Samaritan
woman. He denied Himself to the multitude:
He lay in wait for the individual. This was not
because He undervalued a thousand, it was
because He could not work on the thousand
scale: it was not because He over-valued the
individual, it was because His method was
arranged for the scale of one. Jesus never succeeded in public save once, when He was crucified: He never failed in private save once, with
Pontius Pilate. His method was not sensation:
it was influence. He did not rely on impulses:
He believed in discipline. He never numbered
converts because He knew what was in man:
He sifted them as one winnoweth the wheat
from the chaff. Spiritual statistics are unknown
in the Gospels: they came in with St. Peter in
the pardonable intoxication of success: they
have since grown to be a mania. As the Church
coarsens she estimates salvation by quantity,
how many souls are saved: Jesus was concerned
with quality, after what fashion they were saved.
His mission was to bring Humanity to perfection.

Human nature has been a slow evolution, and Jesus restricted Himself to the highest reaches. He did not say one word on the health of the body, although He is the only man in history that never knew sickness. Health is a matter of physiology: it is assumed in the ideal of Jesus. The Kingdom of God is not meat and drink: it is Righteousness and Peace and Joy. He proposed no rules for the training of the mind and did not condescend to write a book, although every one recognises Jesus as the Prophet of our Race. Mental culture is the province of Literature, and Literature is lower than the highest, for Jesus once cried in a rapture, 'I thank Thee, O Father, Lord of Heaven and earth, because Thou hast hid these things from the wise and prudent and hast revealed them unto babes.' The mind is greater than the body; but there is one place more sacred still where God is enshrined, and the affections, like cherubim, bend over the Will. The Soul is the holiest of all, whose curtains no master dared to raise till Jesus entered as the High Priest of Humanity, and it is in this secret place Jesus works. There are three steps in the Santa Scala which the Race is slowly and painfully

ascending; barbarism where men cultivate the
body, civilisation where they cultivate the intellect, holiness where they cultivate the soul.
There is for the whole Race, for each nation,
for every individual, the age of Homer, the age
of Socrates, the age of Jesus. Beyond the age
of Jesus nothing can be desired or imagined, for
it runs on those lofty tablelands where the soul
lives with God.

Jesus divested Himself of every other interest,
and for three years gave Himself night and day
to the culture of the human soul as a naturalist
to the cultivation of a rare plant, or a scientist to
the conquest of the electric force. He selected
twelve men from the multitude that offered
themselves, whom he considered malleable and
receptive for His discipline. They became His
disciples on whom He lavished labour He could
not afford to the world, and He became their
Master to whom they had committed themselves for treatment. Jesus separated these
men from the world and kept them under
observation night and day: He studied their
failings and idiosyncrasies: He applied His
method in every kind of circumstance and with
calculated degrees of intensity. With a mini-

mum of failure, one out of twelve: with a
maximum of success, eleven men of such
spiritual force that they gave another face to
the world and lifted the Race to its highest
level. The Gospels contain the careful account
of this delicate experiment in religious science,
and Jesus' exposition of the principle of sainthood. Christianity for nineteen centuries has
been the record of its application.

Spiritual culture demands an Ideal as well as
a Discipline, and Jesus availed Himself of the
Ideal of the Prophets. Their chief discovery
was the character of God—when the Hebrew
conscience, the keenest religious instrument in
the ancient world, lifted the veil from the
Eternal, and conceived Jehovah as the imper-
sonation of Righteousness. Their chief service
was the insistence on the duty of Righteousness—who placed in parallel columns the
characters of God and man, and dared to believe
that every man ought to be the replica of God.
Their text was the Holy One,—their endless
and unanswerable sermon, Holiness. Jesus
adopted the obligation of Holiness, but changed
it into a Gospel by revealing the latent relationship between man and God. Had one

asked the Hebrew Prophet, Why ought I to be holy? he had replied at his best, because Holiness is the law of your being. Jesus accepted the law, but added, because a son ought to be like his Father. The Law without became an instinct within. Holiness is conformity to type, and the one standard of perfection is God Himself. Set the soul at liberty, and its history will be a perpetual approximation to God. 'Be ye holy, for I am holy,' said the Old Testament. 'Be ye perfect, even as your Father which is in Heaven is perfect,' said Jesus.

With a soul that is imperfect, discipline would simply be development. With a soul that is sinful, discipline must begin with deliverance. Jesus, as the Physician of the soul, had not merely to do with growth: He had to deal with deformity; and Jesus, who alone has analysed sin, has alone prescribed its cure. Before Jesus, people tried to put away sin by the sacrifice of bulls and goats, and so exposed themselves to the merciless satire of the Prophets; since Jesus, people have imagined that they could be loosed from their sins by the dramatic spectacle of Jesus' death, and so have made the crucifixion of none effect. If sin be a principle in a man's life, than it is evident that it cannot be affected by the most pathetic act in history exhibited from without; it must be met by an opposite principle working from within. If sin be selfishness, as Jesus taught, then it can only be overcome by the introduction of a spirit of self-renunciation. Jesus did not denounce sin: negative religion is always impotent. He replaced sin by virtue, which is a silent revolution. As the light enters, the darkness departs, and as soon as one renounced himself, he had ceased from sin.

Jesus placed His disciples under an elaborate and calculated regimen, which was intended at every point to check the fever of self-will, and reduce the swollen proportions of our lower self. They were to repress the petty ambitions of society. 'When thou art bidden of any man to a wedding, sit not down in the highest room . . . but when thou art bidden, go and sit down in the lowest room.' They were to mortify the self-importance and vain dignity that will not render commonplace kindness. 'If I then, your Lord and Master, have washed your feet, ye also ought to wash one another's feet.' They were not to wrangle about place, or seek after great things. 'Jesus took a child, and set him by Him, and said unto them, . . . he that is least among you all, the same shall be great.' They were not to insist on rights and resist injustice fiercely. 'Whosoever shall smite thee on thy right cheek, turn to him the other also. And if any man will sue thee at the law, and take away thy coat, let him have thy cloke also.' Jesus once cast into keen contrast the life of the world, which one was inclined to follow, and the life of the Kingdom His disciples must achieve. 'Ye know that they which are accounted to rule over the Gentiles exercise lordship over them; and their great ones exercise authority upon them'—that is the self-life where men push and rule. 'But so shall it not be among you: but whosoever shall be great among you, shall be your minister'—this is the selfless life where men submit and serve.

Jesus' regimen had two degrees. The first was self-denial; the second was suffering, which is self-denial raised to its full strength. If a young man really desired to possess 'ageless life,' he must sell all he had and give to the poor. If a publican desired the Kingdom of

God, he must leave all and follow Jesus. Men might have to abandon everything they possessed and every person they loved, for Jesus' sake and the Gospel's. The very instincts of nature must be held in check, and at times laid on the altar. 'He that loveth father and mother more than Me is not worthy of Me, and he that loveth son or daughter more than Me is not worthy of Me.' This was not the senseless asceticism that supposed life could be bought with money, and it was still less the jealousy of a master that grudged any affection given to another. It was the illustration of that Selflessness which is the Law of Holiness, the enforcement of that death which is the gate of Life. It was the exposition of Jesus' famous paradox, 'He that findeth his life shall lose it, and he that loseth his life for My sake shall find it.' Behold His discipline of perfection, upon which in a moment of fine inspiration Jesus conferred the name of the Cross. The Cross is the symbol of self-renunciation and self-sacrifice, and is Jesus' method of salvation. If any one desires to be saved by Jesus, this is how he is going to be saved. It is the 'Secret of Jesus': the way which He has Himself trod, and by which He leads His disciples unto God. ' If any man will come after Me, let him deny himself, and take up his cross and follow Me.'

The Cross was an open secret to the first disciples, and they climbed the steep ascent to Heaven by the ' Royal Way of the Holy Cross,' but its simplicity has been often veiled in later days. Perhaps the simplicity of the symbol has cast a glamour over the modern mind and blinded us to its strenuous meaning. Art, for instance, with an unerring instinct of moral beauty, has seized the Cross and idealised it. It is wrought in gold and hung from the neck of light-hearted beauty; it is stamped on the costly binding of Bibles that go to church in carriages; it stands out in bold relief on churches that are filled with easy-going people. Painters have given themselves to crucifixions, and their striking works are criticised by persons who praise the thorns in the crown, but are not quite pleased with the expression on Jesus' face, and then return to their pleasures. Composers have cast the bitter Passion of Jesus into stately oratorios, and fashionable audiences are affected unto tears. Jesus' Cross has been taken out of His hands and smothered in flowers : it has become what He would have hated, a source of graceful ideas and agreeable emotions. When Jesus presented the Cross for the salvation of His disciples, He was certainly not thinking of a sentiment, which can disturb no man's life, nor redeem any man's soul, but of the unsightly beam which must be set up in the midst of a man's pleasures, and the jagged nails that must pierce his soul.

Theological science has also shown an unfortunate tendency to monopolise the Cross, till the symbol of salvation has been lifted out of the ethical setting of the Gospels and planted in an environment of doctrine. The Cross has been too laboriously traced back to decrees and inserted into covenants: it has been too exclusively stated in terms of Justification and Propitiation. This is a misappropriation of the Cross: it is a violation of its purpose. None can belittle the function of the Queen of Sciences or deny her right to theorise regarding the Divine Purposes and the Eternal Righteousness, but it has been a disaster to involve the Cross in these profound speculations. When Theology has said her last word on the Cross it is a mystery to the common people ;

when Jesus says His first word it is a plain path. Jesus did not describe His Cross as a satisfaction to God, else He had hardly asked His disciples to share it ; He always spoke of it as a Regeneration of man, and therefore Jesus declares that if any man be His disciple he must carry it daily. Theology has one territory, which is theory ; Religion has another, which is life, and the Cross belongs to Religion. The Gospels do not represent the Cross as a judicial transaction between Jesus and God, on which He throws not the slightest light, but as a new force which Jesus has introduced into life, and which He prophesies will be its redemption. The Cross may be made into a doctrine ; it was prepared by Jesus as a discipline.

There are two methods of healing for the body, and they are not on the same moral level. One physician prescribes a medicine whose ingredients are unknown, and whose operation is instantaneous, which is certain for all and the same for all. The patient swallows it and is cured without understanding and without co-operation. This is cure by magic, and is very suspicious. Another physician makes his diagnosis and estimates the symptoms, selects his remedy in correspondence with the disease, and takes his patient into his confidence. He enlists one's intelligence, saying, You must have this medicine, because you have that disease. There is no secrecy, for there is nothing to hide : there is no boasting, for so much depends on the patient. This is cure by science. There are two kinds of Religion for the relief of man. One offers a formula to be accepted and swallowed. It may be in the form of a sacrament, or of a text, or of a view. But as soon as the person receives it without doubt, he is saved. If he wishes to understand the How of the operation, he is assured that it is an incomprehensible mystery. Here there is no connection with reason, no action of the Will. It is salvation by magic. The other religion makes a careful analysis of sin, and proposes a course of treatment which a man can understand and apply. It is an antidote to the poison acting directly and gradually, in perfect harmony with the laws of human nature. Is one willing to make a trial? then he can enter into its meaning and test its success. This is salvation by science, and it is not the least of the excellences in Jesus' method that it is grounded on reason and can be tried by experience. The action of the Cross on sin is as simple in its higher sphere as the reduction of fever by antipyrine or of inflammation by a counter-irritant in physical disease.

Jesus does not appeal to authority for the sanction of His method—always a hazardous resort. He rests on facts which lie to every one's hands. Self-examination is the vindication of the Cross. Is not every man conscious of a strange duality, so that he seems two men? There is the self who is proud, envious, jealous—a lower self. There is the self which is modest, generous, ungrudging—a higher self. Just as the lower self is repressed the higher lives; just as the lower is pampered the higher dies. We are conscious of this conflict and desire that the evil self be crushed, mortified, killed; that the better self be liberated, fed, developed. It goes without saying that the victory of the evil self would be destruction, that the victory of the better self would be salvation. It is at this point Jesus comes in with His principle of self-renunciation. If any man will place himself under My direction, says

Jesus, and take the rule from Me, ' let him deny himself, and take up his cross and follow Me.' As Peter would thrice deny his Lord, so must Jesus' disciple at all times deny his old self and refuse to know it. The habit of self-renunciation is the crucifixion of sin.

It were, however, a depreciation of the Cross to limit it to a remedy for sin : it is also, in Jesus' mind, a discipline of perfection for the soul. It is more than a deliverance, it is an entrance into the life of God. The Cross is not only the symbol for the life of man, it is equally the symbol for the life of God, and it may indeed be said that the Cross is in the heart of God. Jesus has taught us that the equivalent of life is sacrifice, and it is with God that sacrifice begins. ' God so loved the world that He gave His only begotten Son,' said Jesus with profound significance, for His coming was the revelation of the Divine nature. The Incarnation was an act of sacrifice, so patent and so brilliant that it has arrested every mind. It was sacrifice unto the lowest and therefore life in the highest, an outburst and climax of Life. But Creation is also Sacrifice, since it is God giving Himself; and Providence is Sacrifice,

since it is God revealing Himself. Grace is
Sacrifice, since it is God girding Himself and
serving. With God, as Jesus declares Him,
Life is an eternal procession of gifts, a costly
outpouring of Himself, an unwearied suffering
of Love. To live is to love, to love is to suffer,
and to suffer is to rejoice with a joy that fills
the heart of God from age to age. The mystery
of Life, Divine and human, possibly the mystery
of the Holy Trinity, is contained in these words
of Jesus : ' Verily, verily, I say unto you, except
a corn of wheat fall into the ground it abideth
alone, but if it die it bringeth forth much fruit.
He that loveth his life shall lose it ; and he that
hateth his life in this world shall keep it unto
life eternal.' The development of the soul is
along the way of the Cross to the heights of
life. As one of the mystics has it, ' A life of
carelessness is to nature and the self and the
Me the sweetest and pleasantest, but it is not
the best, and to some men may become the
worst. Though Christ's life be the most bitter
of all, yet it is to be preferred above all.' ' What,'
asks Herder, ' has close fellowship with God
ever proved to man but a costly, self-sacrificing
service ?' What else could it be if Love is

the law of spiritual Life throughout the universe?

Progress by suffering is one of Jesus' most characteristic ideas, and, like every other, is embodied in the economy of human nature and confirmed by the sweep of human history. The Cross marks every departure : the Cross is the condition of every achievement. Modern Europe has emerged from the Middle Ages, Christianity from Judaism, Judaism from Egypt, Egypt from barbarism, with throes of agony. Humanity has fought its way upwards at the point of the bayonet, torn and bleeding, yet hopeful and triumphant. As each nation suffers, it prospers; as it ceases to suffer, it decays. Our England was begotten in the sore travail of Elizabeth's day. The American nation sprang from the sons of martyrs. United Germany was baptised in blood. The pioneers of science have lived hardly. The most original philosopher of modern times ground glasses for a living, and was the victim of incurable disease. The master poem of English speech was written by a blind and forsaken Puritan. The New World was found in spite of a hostile court and treacherous friends.

Some have imagined an earthly paradise for the race, where it would have remained ignorant of good and evil, without exertion, without hardship. Jesus saw with clearer eyes. He made no moan over a lost Eden, He knew that it is a steep road that leads to the stars. Jesus believed that the price of all real life is suffering, and that a man must sell all that he has to buy the pearl of great price. Twice at least He lifted this experience into a law. 'Enter ye in at the strait gate . . . because strait is the gate and narrow is the way which leadeth unto life.' And again, after His glowing eulogy on John in His intensity : ' From the days of John the Baptist until now the kingdom of heaven suffereth violence, and the violent take it by force.'

Jesus Himself remains for ever the convincing illustration of this severe culture. His rejection by a wicked generation and the outrages heaped upon Him seemed an unredeemed calamity to the disciples. His undeserved and accumulated trials were at times a burden almost too great for Jesus' own soul. But He entered into their meaning before the end, because they were bringing His Humanity to the fulness of perfection. Without His Cross Jesus had been poorer in the world this day and might have been unloved. It was suffering that wrought in Him that beauty of holiness, sweetness of patience, wealth of sympathy, and grace of compassion, which constitute His divine attraction, and are seating Him on His throne. Once when the cloud fell on Him, He cried, 'Father, save me from this hour'; when the cloud lifted, Jesus saw of the travail of His soul—'I, if I be lifted up from the earth, will draw all men unto Me.' In the upper room Jesus was cast down for an instant; then Iscariot went out to arrange for the arrest, and Jesus revived at the sight of the Cross: 'Now is the Son of Man glorified.' Two disciples are speaking of the great tragedy as they walk to Emmaus, when the risen Lord joins them and reads the riddle of His Life. It was not a disaster: it was a design. 'Ought not Christ to have suffered these things, and to enter into His glory?' The Perfection of Jesus was the fruit of the Cross.

'Thou must go without, go without—that is the everlasting song which every hour all our life through hoarsely sings to us'—is the profound utterance of a great teacher; but Jesus has said it better in His commandment of self-abnegation and His offer of the Cross. It has been the custom to make a contrast between John the Baptist with his stern *régime* and Jesus with His gentle Gospel, but the difference was in spirit, not in method. If the religion of John was strenuous, so was the religion of Jesus. It is a necessity of the spiritual world Jesus Himself could not break. Hardness is of the essence of Religion, like the iron band within the golden crown. Jesus was willing to undertake the culture of every man's soul, but He knew no other way than the Cross. If His disciples wished to sit on His throne, they must drink His cup and be baptised with His baptism. Jesus did not walk one way Himself and propose another for the disciples, but invited them to His experience if they desired His attainment. His method was not the materialistic cross of Munkàcsy, it was the mystical cross of Perugino. Jesus nowhere commanded that one cling to His Cross, He everywhere commanded that one carry His Cross, and out of this daily crucifixion has been born the most beautiful

sainthood from St. Paul to St. Francis, from
À Kempis to George Herbert. For 'there is
no salvation of the soul nor hope of everlasting
life but in the Cross.'

FAITH THE SIXTH SENSE

VII

FAITH THE SIXTH SENSE

Religion is recognised not only as a universal factor in human history, but also as an essential element of human nature, so that if any person with a sense of responsibility proposes to remove the supernatural Religion of the past, he feels himself bound to replace it with a natural Religion for the future. It is one thing however to do homage to a ruler, it is another to identify his throne, and, apart from Jesus, it were hardly possible to determine the seat of Religion. Some have argued that Religion is the fulfilment of duty; this is to settle Religion in the conscience and to reduce it to morality. Some have insisted that Religion is the acceptance of revealed truth; this is to settle Religion in the reason, and to resolve Religion into knowledge. Some have pleaded that Religion is a state of feeling; this is to settle Religion in the heart and to dissolve it into emotion. The philosopher, the theologian, the mystic can each make out a good case, for each has without doubt represented a side of Religion. None of the three can exclude the other two; all three cannot include Religion. Piety, knowledge, emotion are only prolegomena to Religion— its favourite forms and customs. Localise Religion in any of those spheres, and you have a provincial notion; what we want is an imperial idea of our greatest experience. As usual, we owe it to Jesus.

Jesus recognised the variety of the religious spirit and gave His direct sanction to its choice fruits. Religion is obedience to the highest law: 'Ye are My friends if ye do whatsoever I command you.' Religion is knowledge: 'that they might know Thee, the only true God, and Jesus Christ whom Thou hast sent.' Religion is a sublime emotion: 'She hath washed My feet with tears, and wiped them with the hairs of her head.' But religion with Jesus is not merely an influence diffused through our spiritual nature like heat through iron; it has a separate existence. Religion is not a nomad that has to receive hospitality in some foreign department of the soul; it has its own home and habitation. It is a faculty of our constitution as much as Conscience or Reason, with its own sphere of operations and peculiar function. When some exuberant writer refers to Religion as a fungoid growth or a decaying superstition, one is amazed at his belated state of mind. Science discovers that Religion has shaped the past of the Race, and concludes that it will always be a factor in its evolution. Jesus did not create Religion, it is a human instinct. He defined it, and Jesus' synonym for the faculty of Religion is Faith.

Jesus as the Prophet of Religion was ready to submit every word of His teaching to Conscience and Reason. He never suggested that what would have been immoral in man might be moral in God. His argument was ever from the good in man to the best in God. Human fatherhood was a faint suggestion of Divine Fatherhood. 'What man is there of you, whom if his son ask bread, will he give him a stone? . . . If ye then, being evil, know how to give good gifts unto your children, how much more shall your Father which is in Heaven give good things to them that ask Him?' He

never insisted that what was absolutely incredible to man was therefore all the more
likely to be true with God, but used the human
as the shadow of the divine. Common sense in
man was Grace in God. 'What man of you,
having an hundred sheep, if he lose one of them,
doth not leave the ninety and nine in the wilderness, and go after that which is lost till he
find it?' Jesus claimed no exemption for His
doctrine from the Law of Righteousness or the
Law of Fitness, but it was in another court He
chose to state His case for decision.

When Jesus made His chief appeal to the individual He addressed Himself to Faith. He
asked many things of men, but the first and last
duty was to believe. Faith lay behind life; it
formed character, it inspired discipline. 'What
shall we do,' said captious Jews, 'that we might
work the works of God?' Jesus answered and
said unto them, 'This is the work of God, that
ye believe on Him whom He hath sent.' Before
the soul came to perfection it would have to
suffer, but it must begin by believing, else there
could be no Religion. Jesus' mind was continually fixed on Faith; the word was ever on
His lips. It was the recurring decimal of His

thinking, the keynote of His preaching. His
custom was to divide men into classes from the
standpoint of Religion, not morals—those who
believed, those who believed not. He marvelled
twice: once at men's unbelief, once at a Roman
centurion's faith. When any one sought His
help He demanded faith. When He rebuked
His disciples it was usually because they had
little faith. Understand what Jesus meant by
Faith and you understand what Jesus meant by
Religion.

Just as a ship is kept in the waterway by the
buoys on either side, so does one arrive at
Jesus' idea of Faith by grasping the startling
fact that it was quite different from the idea of
His own day. The contemporary believer of
Jesus was a Pharisee, and his faith stood in the
passionate acceptance of a national tradition.
He believed that the Jewish nation was the
exclusive people of God, and that Jerusalem
would yet be the metropolis of the world, with
a thousand inferences and regulations that had
grown like fungi on the trunk of this stately
hope. It was contrary to fact to say a Pharisee
believed in God: it came out that he did not
know God when he saw Him. It is correct to

say that he believed in a dogma which, in another age, might have been that of the Holy Trinity, but in his age happened to be that of the national destiny. The dogma of the monopoly of God was difficult to hold, being vulnerable both from the side of God and man. Jesus Himself showed that it did not correspond with the nature of God, whose mercy was not a matter of ethnology. 'I tell you of a truth ... many lepers were in Israel in the time of Eliseus the prophet, and none of them was cleansed, saving Naaman the Syrian.' He pointed out that it was contradicted by the nature of man, whose piety was not a matter of geography. 'I say unto you, That many shall come from the east and west, and shall sit down with Abraham, Isaac, and Jacob in the kingdom of Heaven.' While this dogma had the advantage of being patriotic, it had the misfortune of being incredible to any fair-minded and reasonable person. You could only believe it by shutting your eyes to facts, and making the most intolerable assumptions. Faith with a Pharisee was the opposite of Reason.

Jesus also had a contrast in the background of His mind, and it throws His idea of Faith

into bold relief. 'Master,' said certain of the
Scribes and Pharisees to Jesus, 'we would see a
sign from Thee.' It was dangerous, they considered, to let truth stand on her merits: for a
prophet to rest his claim on his character. It
was safer to shift from truth to miracles and to
depend on the intervention of the supernatural.
Jesus was angry because this wanton demand
for a sign was the tacit denial of Faith, and the
open confession of an irreligious heart. 'An
evil and adulterous generation,' He said, 'seek-
eth after a sign.' A nobleman was impressed
by the spiritual power of Jesus, and besought
Him to heal his sick son. His faith was strong
enough to believe that Jesus could do this good
work; it was too weak to believe that Jesus
could work at a distance. Faith in this man's
mind was fettered by conditions of sight, and so
was less than faith. 'Except,' said Jesus, 'ye
see signs and wonders ye will not believe.'
When Jesus rose from the dead He found that
one of His apostles had not kept Easter Day,
and would not accept His Resurrection unless
Jesus afforded him physical proof of the most
humble and elementary kind. Jesus conceded
to Love what could not be given to faith, and

St. Thomas, who had lost faith in Jesus' humanity, rose to the faith of His divinity. But Jesus reproached him, and rated his faith at a low value. It was only a bastard faith that had not freed itself of sight. 'Because thou hast seen Me, thou hast believed: blessed are they that have not seen and yet have believed.' 'What,' said St. Augustine, 'is Faith, but to believe what you do not see?' It was a happy epitome of the teaching of Jesus. With Jesus Faith is the opposite of sight.

Jesus crystallised the idea of Faith which is held in solution throughout the Bible, and rests on the assumption of two worlds. There is the physical world which lies round us on every side, and of which our bodies are a part. This is one environment, and the instrument of knowledge here is sight. There is the spiritual world which is hidden by the veil of the physical, and of which our souls are a part. This is another environment, and the instrument of knowledge here is faith. There is an order in the education of Humanity, and the first lesson is not faith but sight. The race, and each individual in his turn, begins with the experience of the physical: seeing visible objects, handling material possessions, hearing audible voices, looking at flesh-and-blood people. It is a new and hard lesson to realise the spiritual: to enter into the immaterial, inaudible, invisible, intangible life of the soul; to catch a voice that only calls within, to follow a mystical presence through a trackless wilderness, to wait for an inheritance that eye hath not seen, to store our treasure on the other side of the grave. This is to leave our kindred and our father's house, and to go into a land which God will show us. It is to emerge from the physical, it is to enter into the spiritual sphere. It is an immense advance; it is a tremendous risk. Any one who shifts the centre of his life from the world which is seen to the world which is unseen deserves to be called a believer. Abraham was the first man in history who dared to make this venture and to cast himself on God. He discovered the new world of the soul, and is to this day the father of the faithful.

Jesus insisted on Faith for the same reason that a mathematician relies on the sense of numbers, or an artist on the sense of beauty: it was the one means of knowledge in His department. He was the Prophet of God and

must address the God-faculty in man. Between
Faith and God there was the same correspondence as between the eye and light. Faith
proves God : God demands Faith. When any
one ignored Faith and fell back on sight in the
quest for God Jesus was in despair. Before
such wilful stupidity He was amazed and helpless. You want to see, was His constant
complaint, when in the nature of things you
must believe. There is one sphere where sight
is the instrument of knowledge : use it there—
it is not my sphere. There is another where
faith is the instrument; use it there—that
is my sphere. But do not exchange your
instruments. You cannot see what is spiritual;
you might as well expect to hear a picture.
What you see you do not believe; it is a mis-
nomer; you see it. What you believe you
cannot see; it would be an absurdity; you
believe it. Faith is the instinct of the spiritual
world: it is the sixth sense—the sense of the
unseen. Its perfection may be the next step
in the evolution of the Race.

Jesus continually offered Himself as the
object of Faith because He was the Revelation
of the unseen world. Believe on Me, He said

with authority, not on the ground that He was God, whom no man could see, but because He was sent by God, whom He declared. 'Shew us the Father and it sufficeth us,' was the confused cry of Faith. 'He that hath seen Me hath seen the Father,' was Jesus' answer. To see Jesus was not sight: it was Faith. Sight only showed a Jewish peasant, and therefore Jesus said once to the Jews, 'Ye also have seen Me and believe not.' Faith detected His veiled glory; therefore Jesus said to St. Peter on his great confession, 'Flesh and blood hath not revealed it unto thee, but my Father which is in Heaven.' Jesus did not depend on His metaphysical equality with the Father, but on His moral likeness to the Father—not on His eternal generation, but on His spiritual character. Reason must decide whether Jesus be God and Man in two distinct natures and one person: it is the function of faith to respond to His Divine excellence, who was

> 'Fulfilled with God-head as a cup
> Filled with a precious essence.'

God was made visible and beautiful to Faith as Jesus spoke and worked, and the denial of Jesus was the denial of God. 'The Father

Himself, which hath sent Me, hath borne witness of Me. Ye have neither heard His voice at any time nor seen His shape; and ye have not His word abiding in you, for Whom He hath sent ye believe not.' Faith fulfils itself in the discovery and acceptance of Jesus; beyond him nothing is to be desired, no one to be imagined. As Mr. T. H. Green says, 'Faith is the communication of the Divine Spirit by which Christ as the revealed God dwells in our heart. It is the awakening of the Spirit of Adoption whereby we cry, Abba, Father.'

Two questions which harass the religious mind in our day were never anticipated by Jesus' hearers: they were impossible under His idea of Faith. When Faith is an isolated and subtle act of the soul, some will always ask, What is Faith? and some will always reply, There are seven kinds, more or less, and the end will be hopeless confusion. If Faith be defined as the sense of the unseen which detects, recognises, loves, and trusts the goodness existing in numerous forms and persons in the world, and rises to its height in trusting Him who is its source and sum, then it is needless to inquire, 'What is Faith?' We are walking

by Faith in one world every day with our souls,
as we are walking by sight in another world
with our bodies. No one asked Jesus, 'How
can Faith be obtained?' because Jesus did not
regard Faith as an arbitrary gift of the Almighty, or an occasional visitant to favoured
persons, but as one of the senses of the soul.
Jesus did not divide men into those who had
Faith and those who had not, but into those
who used the faculty, and those who refused to
use it. He expected people to believe when He
presented evidence, as you expect one to look if
you show him a picture. One might have weak
faith as one might have short sight: one might
be faithless as one might be blind. That is
beside the question. The Race has sight, although a few may be blind, and the Race has
Faith, although a few may not believe.

Jesus regarded the feeblest effort of this
faculty with hope because it lifted the soul
above the limitations of this life and allied it to
the Eternal. 'With God all things are possible,'
and therefore, 'If thou canst believe, all things
are possible to him that believeth.' When His
disciples caught a glimpse of the higher life and
prayed 'Increase our Faith,' Jesus encouraged

them. 'If ye had Faith as a grain of mustard
seed (synonym for smallness), ye might say unto
this sycamine tree (synonym for greatness), Be
thou plucked up by the root, and be thou
planted in the sea ; and it should obey you. It
was not easy to believe strongly any more than
to see far, and Faith, like any other faculty,
must be trained by discipline. Jesus was evidently satisfied with the father who said with
tears, 'Lord, I believe ; help Thou mine unbelief,' and ever cast His protection over struggling Faith. Positive unbelief or absolute in-
capacity of Faith, Jesus refused to pity or con-
done. It was not a misfortune : it was a wilful
act. It was atrophy through misuse or neglect,
and was, to His mind, sin.

This judgment would be a gross injustice if
Faith were an accomplishment of saints ; it is
an inevitable conclusion if Faith be an inherent
faculty. No one could be reduced to this helpless state unless he had habitually shut his
soul against the unseen as it lapped him round
and had fastened his whole interest on this
world. It was one of the paradoxes of Jesus'
day, that the same people were the conventional
believers and the typical unbelievers. The

Pharisees believed in their creed with pathetic tenacity and disbelieved in Jesus with hopeless obstinacy, and the reason of their faith and their unbelief was the same. It was their utter and unqualified worldliness. They believed in a kingdom where its citizens strove for the chief seats of the synagogues and the highest rooms at feasts; they were offended with a kingdom whose type was a little child and whose Messiah came to serve. They had lived so long in the dark of vain ambition and material aims, that their eye-balls had withered, and when they came into the open they could not see. 'How can ye believe,' said Jesus to the Jews, illuminating at one stroke His idea of Faith and the reason of their unbelief, 'which receive honour one of another, and seek not the honour that cometh from God only?'

Jesus' attitude to miracles hangs on His idea of Faith. Define Faith as the antagonist of reason, and miracles are then a necessity. They are the twelve legions of angels which intervene on the side of Truth. Define Faith as the supplement to reason in the sphere of the unseen, and miracles are at best a provisional assistance. If faith had been alert and strong,

K

then miracles had been an incumbrance. Since Faith was weak and inert, miracles served a purpose. For a moment the spiritual order projected itself into the natural and arrested attention. No one could deny another state, and he might be roused to possess it. A miracle was a sign, a lightning flash that proves the electricity in the air; otherwise a useless and alarming phenomenon to men. Jesus did not think highly of physical miracles; He was annoyed when they were asked; He wrought them with great reserve; He depreciated their spiritual value on all occasions. If blind men could not see the light, let them have the lightning, but it was a poor makeshift. 'If I do not the works of My father, believe me not. But if I do, though ye believe not Me (recognize Me), believe the works, that ye may know and believe that the Father is in Me and I in Him.' So He put it to the Jews, and His heart sometimes failed Him about His own disciples. 'Believe Me that I am in the Father and the Father in Me: or else believe Me for the very works' sake.'

' You stick a garden-plot with ordered twigs,
To show inside lie germs of herbs unborn,

And check the careless step would spoil their birth :
But when herbs wave, the guardian twigs may go.
. . .   This book's fruit is plain,
Nor miracles need prove it any more.'

Jesus was Himself the one convincing and
permanent miracle, the 'avenue into the unseen.' When any one believes in Jesus he has
the key of revelation and the vision of Heaven.
' Because I said unto thee, I saw thee under the
fig tree, believest thou? thou shalt see greater
things than these. And He saith unto him,
Verily, verily, I say unto you, hereafter ye
shall see Heaven open, and the angels of God
ascending and descending upon the Son of
man.'

With Jesus' idea of faith religion is independent of external evidence, and carries a warrant
in her own bosom. The foundation of Faith is
a grave problem, and its difficulty is admirably
raised in an Eastern legend. The world rests on
an elephant. Very good : and the elephant itself
on a tortoise : and the tortoise ? on air—sooner
or later you come to air—no foundation. There
are two conceivable grounds on which Faith can
stablish herself, and each is a priceless assistance.
One is the testimony of faithful people in all

the ages; this is an infallible Church. The
other is that 'volume which is a Divine supplement to the laws of nature and of conscience': this is an infallible Book. But what
is to certify the Church or the Book? Their
character alone can be their certificate, and how
am I to identify this character save by my
Faith? We end where we began—with Faith,
which must be self-verifying and self-sustaining.
We believe in Jesus, not because the prophets
anticipated Him or disciples have magnified
Him, but, in the last issue, because He is such
an one as we must believe. Jesus is the justification because He is the satisfaction of Faith.
Faith is thankful for every aid, and strengthens
herself on the Bible, but Faith is self-sufficient.
'In its true nature,' to quote Mr. Green again,
'Faith can be justified by nothing but itself,'
or, as John Baptist has it, 'What He hath seen
and heard, that He testifieth . . . he that
hath received His testimony hath set to his
seal that God is true.'

Jesus' idea of Faith explained His contradictory attitude to this visible world, which was
sometimes one of friendliness, sometimes one of
watchfulness. When He saw the world as the

shadow of the real, He loved it and wove it into an endless parable. Its fertility, tenderness, richness, brilliancy were all signs of the Kingdom of Heaven fulfilled in Himself. 'I am the true vine;' 'I am the good Shepherd'; 'I am the Light of the world'; He was the 'living water.' He was the substance of every appearance: the truth under every form. The spiritual was embodied in this world, as Jesus was God in human flesh, and he that believed, like St. John, could see. This was the appreciation of the world. When Jesus thought of the world as the veil of the spiritual, He was concerned, and warned His disciples lest they should be caught by the glitter of the visible, lest they should be held in the prison of the material. They must have a sense of proportion, seeking first the Kingdom of God and His righteousness: they must not fret about this world, knowing it to be an appendage of the Kingdom. They ought not to lay up for themselves treasures on earth, because they would be lost; they must store their treasures in heaven, because they would last. They ought not to fear the trials of this life, because persecution cannot injure the soul; they ought to fear spiritual disaster only, because it is destruction to be cast into hell fire. He that seeks to house his soul in barns is a fool; he that prepares an everlasting dwelling-place is wise. The world as a parable is perfect; as a possession it is worthless. It is never to be compared with the soul, or the kingdom of God. Jesus did not denounce the world as wicked, He disparaged it as unreal. This is the depreciation of the world.

When Jesus' idea of faith is accepted, then its province in human life will be finally delimitated, and various frontier wars brought to an end. Painters will still give us charming pictures of Faith and Reason, but they will no longer represent Reason as a mailed knight picking his way from stone to stone, while Faith as a winged angel floats by his side. Faith and Reason will be neighbouring powers, each absolute in its own region. It is the part of Reason to verify intellectual conceptions and apply intellectual principles, and Faith must not disturb this work. It is the part of Faith to gather those hopes and feelings which lie outside the intellect, and Faith must not be hampered by Reason. When the knight comes to the edge of the cliff, he can go no farther;

then Faith, like Angelico's San Michele, opens his strong wings and passes out in the lonely quest for God. An Eastern has understood Jesus perfectly. 'What Reason is to things demonstrable,' he says, 'is Faith to the invisible realities of the spirit world.'

One may also hope that with Christian views of Faith we shall not hear any more of a recon-ciliation between Science and Religion, which is as if you proposed to reconcile Geology and Astronomy. Science has, for its field, everything material; religion, everything spiritual. When the scientist comes, as he constantly does, on something beyond his tests, as, for instance, life, he ought to leave it to Religion. When the saint comes on something material, as, for instance, creation, he ought to leave it to Science. Faith has no apparatus for science; science has no method of discovering God. For the phenomena of the universe we look to Science; for the facts of the soul to Faith. 'A division as old as Aristotle,' say the authors of the *Unseen Universe*, 'separates speculators into two great classes: those who study the How of the universe, and those who study the Why. All men of Science are embraced in the former of these; all men of Religion in the latter.'

Define Faith as the Religious faculty, and you at once lift from its shoulders the burden of Theology. In the minds of many, Faith and Religion have been so confounded together as to be practically one, and Faith has been exercised on dogmas when it should have been resting in God. Theology is a Science; it is created by reason. Religion is an experience; it is guided by faith. The Catholic doctrine of the Trinity, for instance, is a very elaborate effort of reason, and is not, strictly speaking, within the scope of faith. When one says 'I believe' in the Nicene Creed, one means that he assents to the theological statement. When one says 'Lord, I believe' in Jesus' sense, one means that he trusts—a very different thing. Jesus' physical Resurrection, in the same way, is a question that can only be decided by evidence, and is within the province of reason. His spiritual Resurrection is a drama of the soul, and a matter of faith. When I declare my belief that on the third day Jesus rose, I am really yielding to evidence. When I am crucified with Christ, buried with Christ, and rise to newness of life in

Christ, I am believing after the very sense of Jesus.

Our wisdom in this day of confusion is to extricate Faith from all entanglements, and exercise the noblest, surest, strongest faculty of our nature on Jesus Christ, whose Person constitutes the evidence of the unseen, whose one demand on all men is Trust, whose promise, fulfilled to an innumerable multitude, is Rest.

> ' Remember what a martyr said
> On the rude tablet overhead :
> I was born sickly, poor, and mean,
> A slave ; no misery could screen
> The holders of the pearl of price
> From Cæsar's envy ; therefore twice
> I fought with beasts, and three times saw
> My children suffer by his law.
> At last, my own release was earned,
> I was some time in being burned ;
> But at the close a hand came through
> The fire above my head, and drew
> My soul to Christ, whom *now I see*.'

THE LAW OF SPIRITUAL
GRAVITATION

VIII

THE LAW OF SPIRITUAL GRAVITA-
TION

'This is my commandment,' said Jesus, 'that
ye love one another as I have loved you';
'Every particle of matter in the universe,' said
Newton, 'attracts every other particle with a
force directly proportioned to the mass of the
attracting particle, and inversely to the square
of the distance,' are the two monumental de-
liverances in human knowledge, and the Law
of Love in the sphere of metaphysics is the
analogue of the law of gravitation in the sphere
of physics.   The measure of ignorance in
Science has been isolation, when nature appears
a series of unconnected departments.   The
measure of ignorance in Religion has been
selfishness, when the Race appears a certain
number of individuals fighting each for his own
hand.   The master achievement of knowledge

has been the discovery of unity. Before Newton, gravitation was holding the world together;
it was his honour to formulate the law. Before
Jesus, Love was preventing the dissolution of
the Race; it was His glory to dictate the law.
Newton found a number of fragments and left
a physical universe. Jesus found a multitude
of individuals and created a spiritual kingdom.
The advance from a congeries of individuals to
an organised society is marked by four mile-
stones. First, we are simply conscious of other
men and accept the fact of their existence; we
realise our mutual dependence and come to a
working agreement. This is the infancy of the
Race and conscience is not yet awake. Then
we discover that there are certain things one
must not do to his neighbour, and certain ser-
vices one may expect from his neighbour, that
to injure the next man is misery and to help
him is happiness. This is the childhood of the
Race, and conscience now asserts itself. Afterwards we begin to review the situation and to
collect our various duties: we arrange them
under heads and state them in black and white.
This is the youth of the Race, and reason is
now in action. Finally, we take up our list of

black and white rules and try to settle their connection. It is not possible to trace them all to one root and comprehend them in one act? What a light to conscience, a relief to reason, a joy to the heart! This is the mature manhood of the Race, and the heart is now in evidence. From an instinct to duties, from duties to rules, and now from rules to Law. State that Law and the Race becomes one society.

Jesus came at a point of departure; He received the race from Moses and led it into liberty. The Jew of Jesus' day was, in spite of all his limitations, the most spiritual man in the world, and the more thoughtful Jews were sick of a code and thirsting for a principle. 'Master,' said a scribe to Jesus, 'which is the great commandment in the law?' and this anonymous seeker after truth has suffered unjust reproach. He has been imagined a mere pedant held in the bonds of a vain theology, or a cunning sophist anxious to entrap Jesus into a war of words. He ought rather to be thought of as an earnest student whose mind had outgrown a worn-out system, and who was waiting for the new order. His desire was not a puerile comparison of rules; he had tasted the tedium

of such debates in Pharisaic circles: his desire
was to get from the branches to the root. He
believed that Jesus had made the discovery.
Jesue recognised a congenial mind and placed a
generous interpretation on the scribe's words,
' Thou art not far,' He said, ' from the kingdom
of God.'

Jesus addressed Himself to the unity of moral
law in His first great public utterance, and only
concluded His treatment before His arrest in
the garden. His sermon on the mount was a
luminous and comprehensive investigation of
the ten words with a purpose—to detect their
spiritual source and organic connection. It was
the analysis of a code in order to indentify the
principle. It was the experimental search for a
law conducted with every circumstance of
spiritual interest before a select audience; it
was a sustained suggestion by a score of illustrations that the law had been found. Moses
said, ' do this or do that.' Jesus refrained from
regulations—He proposed that we should love.
Jesus, while hardly mentioning the word, planted the idea in His disciples' minds, that Love
was Law. For three years He exhibited and
enforced Love as the principle of life, until,

before he died, they understood that all duty to God and man was summed up in Love. Progress in the moral world is ever from complexity to simplicity. First one hundred duties; afterwards they are gathered into ten commandments; then they are reduced to two: love of God and love of man; and, finally, Jesus says His last word: 'This is My commandment, that ye love one another as I have loved you.'

When Jesus proposes to sum up the whole duty of man in Love, one is instantly charmed with the sentiment, and understands how it made the arid legalism of the scribes to blossom like the rose. How can one conquer sin? How can one come to perfection? How can one have fellowship with God? How can one save the world? And to a hundred questions of this kind Jesus has one answer: 'Love the man next you.' It is the poetry of idealism; it is quite beyond criticism as a counsel of perfection. But we are haunted with the feeling that this is not a serious treatment of the subject. We are inclined to turn from the Galilean dreamer and fall back on the casuists. It is one of our limitations to imagine that poetry is something less than truth instead of its only

L

adequate expression, and that the heart is an impulsive child whose vagaries have to be checked, instead of the imperial power in human nature. We are redeemed in this matter by the inspiration of Jesus. Had Jesus repeated the hackneyed programme of negation with a table of ' shalt nots,' He would have afforded another dreary instance of moral failure. When Jesus published His positive principle of Love, and left each man to draw up his own table, He gave a brilliant pledge of spiritual success. By this magical word of Love He not only brought the dry bones together and made a unity ; He clothed them with flesh and made a living body. He may have forfeited the name of moralist, He has gained the name of Saviour.

Jesus was not an agreeable sentimentalist who imagined that He could cleanse the world by rose-water ; He was the only thinker who grasped the whole situation root and branch. He did not propose to make sin illegal ; that had been done without conspicuous benefit. He proposed to make sin impossible by replacing it with love. If sin be an act of self-will, each person making himself the centre, then Love is the destruction of sin, because love connects instead of isolating. No one can be envious, avaricious, hard-hearted ; no one can be gross, sensual, unclean, if he loves. Love is the death of all bitter and unholy moods of the soul, because Love lifts the man out of himself and teaches him to live in another. Jesus did not think it needful to eulogise the virtues : it would have been a work of supererogation when He had insisted on Love. It is bathos, for instance, to instruct a mother in tenderness; the maternal instinct will fulfil itself. Jesus has changed ethics from a crystal that can only grow by accretion into a living plant that flowers in its season. He exposed the negative principle of morals in His empty house swept and garnished; He vindicated the positive principle in His house held by a strong man armed. The individualism of selfishness is the disintegrating force which has cursed this world, segregating the individual and rending society to pieces. The altruism of Love is the consolidating force which will save the world, reconciling every man to his fellows and recreating society. When Jesus makes Love the basis of social life, He does not need to condescend to details : He has established unity.

When Jesus gave His doctrine of Love in its final form, one is struck by a startling omission. He laid on His disciples the repeated charge of Love to one another, He did not once command them to love God.   While His preachers have in the main exhorted men to love God, Jesus in the main exhorted them to love their fellow-men.   This was not an accident—a bias given to His mind by the immense suffering in the world : it was an intention—the revelation of Jesus' idea of Love.   Conventional religion divides love into provinces—natural love, ranging from the interest of a philanthropist in the poor to the passion of a mother for her child, and spiritual love, whose humblest form is the fellowship of the Christian Church and whose highest is the devotion of the soul to God.   This artifice is the outcome of a limited vision ; it has been published by a contracted heart.   It has ended in the disparagement of natural love and the unreality of spiritual love.   Jesus never once sanctioned this mischievous distinction : He bitterly satirises its effect on conduct.   The Pharisee offers to God the gift which God ought to have gone to his parents' support—so devoted was he to God, so lifted above ordinary affection! Our Master accepted the solidarity of sin, that no one could injure a fellow-creature without hurting God. 'If the world hate you, ye know that it hated Me before it hated you;' and 'He that hateth Me, hateth My Father also.' He accepted with as little reserve the solidarity of Love—that no one could love a fellow-creature with a pure, unselfish passion without loving God. 'He that receiveth you receiveth Me, and he that receiveth Me receiveth Him that sent Me.' As St. John has it, with an echo of past words, 'Beloved, let us love one another: for love is of God; and every one that loveth is born of God.' Life is the school of love, in which we rise from love of mother and wife and child through a long discipline of sacrifice to the love of God. Love is the law of Life.

It was the habit of Jesus' mind to trace the seen at every point into the unseen, and He gave the law of Love its widest and farthest range. He was not content with insisting that the unity of the human stood in Love, He suggested that Love was also the unity of the Divine. The same bond that made one fellowship of St. John and St. Peter was the principle

of communion between the Father and the Son.
With Jesus the Trinity was never a metaphysical
conception—a state of being; it was an ethical
fact—a state of feeling. It was a revelation of
Love which found its life in sacrifice. As the
Father gave the Son, so the Son gave Himself,
and as the Son gave Himself, so must His disciples give themselves for the brethren. God
and Christ were one in love; Christ and man
were one in love. The great Law had full
course, and God and man were united in the
sacrifice of love. 'Therefore doth my Father
love Me, because I lay down My life that I
might take it again. This commandment have
I received of My Father.' 'This is My commandment, that ye love one another as I have
loved you.' 'If ye keep My commandments,
ye shall abide in My love; even as I have kept
My Father's commandments and abide in His
love.' 'If a man love Me, he will keep My
words: and My Father will love him, and we
will come unto him, and make our abode with
him.' Perhaps the most profound symbol of
Jesus was the washing of the disciples' feet, and
therefore the preamble of St. John, 'knowing . . .
that He was come from God and went to God.'

It seemed only an act of lowly and kindly service ; it really was an illustration of the Law which holds in one God Almighty and the meanest man who is inhabited by Jesus' Spirit.

Apart from the Incarnation, which is the theoretical ground of a united humanity, and His Spirit, which is the practical influence working towards that high end, Jesus made two contributions to the cause of unity. He has stated in convincing terms the principle which alone can repair the disruption in society and close its fissures. What rends society in every land is the conflict between the rights of the one and the rights of the many, and harmony can only be established by their reconciliation. Peace can never be made by the suppression of the individual—which is collectivism, nor by the endless sacrifice of a hundred for the profit of one—which is individualism. Jesus came to bring each man's individuality to perfection, not to sink him in the mass. Jesus came to rescue the poor and weak from the tyranny of power and ambition, not to leave them in bondage. Both ends were His, and both are embraced in His new commandment. For the ideal placed before each individual is not rule but service, and in proportion to his attainments will be his sacrifices. By one stroke Jesus secures the welfare of the many who share in the success of the one, and the sanctification of the one whose character is developed by his service of the many. It will not be necessary to cripple any man's power lest it may be a menace to his neighbours, because he will be their voluntary servant, nor will his neighbours be driven to the vice of oppression, because they will not fear. Where Jesus' idea prevails a rivalry of service will be the habit of society, and he will stand highest who stoops lowest in the new order of life.

Jesus also offered in the Church a model of the perfect society, and therefore He established the Church on an eternal and universal principle. Wherever a number of isolated individuals come together and form one body there must be some bond of unity. With a nation it is geography— the people live within certain degrees of latitude. With a party it is opinion—its members bind themselves for a common end. With a firm it is business—its partners trade in the same article. Jesus contemplated a society the most comprehensive and intense, the most elastic and cohesive in history, which would embrace all countries, suit all times, cultivative all varieties, fulfil all aspirations. It was the ambition of Jesus as the Son of Man, and this was the question before His mind: What delicate and pervasive moral system could bind into one the diverse multitude that would call Him Lord, so that I—some obscure nineteenth century Christian—may feel at home in St. Paul's Cathedral, or at St. Peter's, Rome, or in the Metropolitan Church of Athens, or at a Salvation Army meeting? This were indeed an irresistible illustration of spiritual communion and a prophecy of the unity of the Race. 'I belong,' said Angelique, the Abbess of Port Royal, 'to the order of all the saints, and all the saints belong to my order.' What is the bond of this mystical order? Jesus stated and vindicated it in the upper room.

It is the fond imagination of many pious minds that the basis of spiritual unity must lie in the reason, and stand in uniformity of doctrine. This unfortunate idea has been the poisoned spring of all the dissensions that have torn Christ's body from the day when Eastern Christians fought in the streets about His Di-

vinity to the long years when Europe was
drenched in blood about His lovely Sacraments.
It is surely a very ghastly irony that the immense sorrow of the world has been infinitely
increased by the fierce distractions of that society which Jesus intended to be the peace-
maker, and that Christian divisions should have
arisen from the vain effort after an ideal which
Jesus never once had within His vision. With
St. John and St. Thomas, Matthew the publican
and Simon the zealot at the same Holy Table,
it is not likely that Jesus expected one model
of thought: with His profound respect for the
individual and His sense of the variety of
truth, it is certain He did not desire it.

Jesus realised that the tie which binds men
together in life is not forged in the intellect
but in the heart. Behind nations and parties,
behind all the divisions and entanglements of
society stands the family. Love is the first
and the last and the strongest bond in experience. It conquers distance, outlives all changes,
bears the strain of the most diverse opinions.
What a proof of Jesus' divine insight that He
did not make His Church a school—whether of
the Temple or the Porch—but a family: did

not demand in His farewell that His disciples should think alike, but that they should feel alike! He believed it possible to bind men to their fellows on the one condition that they were first bound fast to Him. He made Himself the centre of eleven men, each an independent unit; He sent through their hearts the electric flash of His love and they became one. It was an experiment on a small scale; it proved a principle that has no limits. Unity is possible wherever the current of love runs from Christ's heart through human hearts and back to Christ again. No one is cast out unless he refuse to love: no one is isolated unless he be non-conducting. Within the Church visible, with its wearisome forms and lamentable controversies, lives the Church invisible, the communion of love, and its spirit is a perpetual witness to Christ's mission of atonement: 'That they all may be one; as Thou, Father, art in Me, and I in Thee, that they also may be one in us, that the world may believe that Thou hast sent Me.'

Whenever doctrine and Love have entered the lists, not as friends but as rivals, Love has always won and so has confirmed the wisdom of

Jesus. He has had servants in every country distinguished for their devout spirit and controversial ability. Their generation crowned them for their zeal against heresy, but succeeding generations conferred a worthier immortality. The Church forgot their polemics, she kept their hymns. Bernard of Clairvaux depopulated Europe in order to conquer the Holy Land with the sword for Him who preached peace throughout its borders; but we only remember the saint who wrote :

'Jesus, Thou joy of loving hearts.'

Toplady divided his time between composing hymns instinct with love, and assailing John Wesley with incredible insolence. His acrimonious defence of the Divine Sovereignty is buried and will never be disinterred, but while the Church lasts she will sing

'Rock of ages, cleft for me.'

Rutherford, of St. Andrews, laboured at books of prodigious learning against Prelacy, and the dust lies heavy upon them this day, but the letters he wrote in his prison on the love of Christ have been the delight of Scottish mystics for two centuries. If any one feels compelled to attack a religious neighbour, his contemporaries may call him faithful, his successors will endeavour to forget him. If any one can worthily express the devotion of Christian hearts, his words will pass into the heritage of Christendom. What is not of love, dies almost as soon as it is born : what is of love lives for ever. It has the sanction of Eternal Law; it has in it the breath of immortality.

The Christian consciousness grows slowly into the mind of Jesus. First it clings to legalism with St. Peter; afterwards it learns faith with St. Paul; it enters at last into love with St. John, the final interpreter of Jesus. We are now in the school of St. John, and are beginning to discover that none can be a heretic who loves, nor any one be other than a schismatic who does not love. None can be cast out of God's kingdom if he loves, none received into it if he does not love. Usher cannot excommunicate Rutherford because he was not ordained by a Bishop, nor Rutherford condemn Usher because he was a head and front of Prelacy. Channing cannot exclude Faber because he believes too much, or Faber exclude Channing because he believes too little. None can read Jesus' exposition of Love and imagine such moral disorder. It would be the suspension of spiritual gravitation. We are protected from one another by the Magna Charta of the kingdom : we are under a Law that has no regard to our prejudices. He that loves is blessed ; he that hates is cursed—is the action of an automatic law. It is the very condition of the spiritual world, which is held together by love : it is the very nature of God Himself, who is Love.

> ' I'm apt to think the man
> That could surround the sum of things and spy
> The heart of God and secrets of His Empire
> Would speak but love, with him the bright result
> Would change the hue of intermediate scenes
> And make one thing of all Theology,'

DEVOTION TO A PERSON THE
DYNAMIC OF RELIGION

IX

DEVOTION TO A PERSON THE DYNAMIC OF RELIGION

Nothing is easier than to create a religion; one only needs self-confidence and foolscap paper. An able Frenchman sat down in his study and produced Positivism, which some one pleasantly described as Catholicism minus Christianity. It stimulated conversation in superior circles for years, and only yesterday Mr. Frederic Harrison was explaining to Professor Huxley that this ingenious invention of M. Comte ought to be taken seriously. An extremely clever woman disappeared into Asia and returned with another religion which has distinctly added to the innocent gaiety of the English nation. One never knows when a new religion may not be advertised. Various interesting societies are understood to be working at something, and each novelty receives a

M

good-natured welcome. No person with any sense of humour resents one of these efforts to stimulate the jaded palate of society, unless it be paraded a season too long and threatens to become a bore. Criticism would be absurd: you might as well analyze *Alice in Wonderland*. Comparison with Christianity is impossible: it were an insult to Jesus.

The great religions of the East compel another treatment; one bows before them with wonder and respect. They are not the ephemera of fashion; they are hoar with antiquity. They are not the pastime of a coterie, they have shaped the destinies of innumerable millions. The most profound instinct of the soul breathes in their creeds and clothes itself in their forms, and, notwithstanding their limitations and corruptions, these ancient faiths have each made some contribution to the Race. One has anticipated the self-renunciation of Jesus, another has asserted the mystery of the Eternal, a third has vindicated the unity of God, and a fourth has saturated with filial piety the future rivals of the West. It were unbelief in Divine Providence to deny those faiths a share in the development of humanity: it were inexcusable ignorance to regard them as systems of organised iniquity. They bear traces of noble ancestry, they preserve in their history a record of splendid service. Stricken by time, their ruins affect our imagination like the columns of Karnak. Dying at the heart, these worn-out religions still make more converts than Christianity. No reverent Christian will allow himself to despise the religions of the past; no intelligent Christian doubts that his will be the religion of the future. A child of the East, the religion of Jesus has conquered the West; conceived, as appears, by a Galilean peasant, it has no limitations of thought or custom; with only a minority of the Race, it embraces the dominant nations of the world. The mind of Jesus seems nothing more in the world as yet than a grey dawn; but wise men can see it is the rising sun.

The final test of any religion is its inherent spiritual dynamic: the force of Christianity is the pledge of its success. It is not a school of morals, nor a system of speculation, it is an enthusiasm. This religion is Spring in the spiritual world, with the irresistible charm of the quickening wind and the bursting bud. It is a birth, as Jesus would say, a breath of God that makes all things new. Humanity does not need morals, it needs motives: it is sick of speculation, it longs for action. Men see their duty in every land and age with exasperating clearness. We know not how to do it.

> ' Whom do you count the worst man upon earth,
> Be sure he knows, in his conscience, more
> Of what right is than arrives at birth
> In the best man's acts that we bow before.'

No one condemns the good, he leaves it undone. No one approves the evil, he simply does it. Our moral machinery is complete but motionless. The religion which inspires men with a genuine passion for holiness and a constraining motive of service will last. It has solved the problem of spiritual motion.

Jesus did not create goodness—her fair form had been already carved in white marble by austere hands ; His office was to place a soul within the ribs of death till the cold stone changed into a living body. Before Jesus, goodness was sterile, since Jesus, goodness has blossomed ; He fertilised it with His spirit. It was a theory, it became a force. He took the corn, which had been long stored in the granaries of philosophy, and sowed it in the soft spring earth ; He minted the gold and made it current coin. Christianity is in Religion what steam is in mechanics, the power which drives. Jesus wrote nothing, He said little, but He did what He said and made others do as He commanded. His religion began at once to exist; from the beginning it was a life. It is the distinction of Christianity that it goes. This is why some of us, in spite of every intellectual difficulty, must believe Jesus to be the Son of God—He has done what no other ever did, and what only God could do. He is God because He discharges a 'God-function.'

> ' 'Tis one thing to know and another to practise,
> And thence I conclude that the real God-function
> Is to furnish a motive and injunction,
> For practising what we know already.'

Religion with Jesus has a dynamic, and it is Jesus Himself, for Jesus and His religion are as soul and body. He did not evolve it as an intellectual conception, He exhibited it as a state of life. It was never a paper scheme like Plato's *Republic* or More's *Utopia*. Jesus' religion was in life before it appeared in the Gospels ; it had been fulfilled in Himself before it was preached to the world. The Gospels are not only a programme, they are already a history. Christianity has been apt to sink into a creed or a ceremony—it is the decadence of Pharisaism—in Jesus' hand it was a life. Jesus never proposed that men should discuss His Gospel, He invited men to live it. 'Whosoever cometh to Me, and heareth My sayings and doeth them . . . is like a man which built an house . . . on a rock.' He did not suggest lines of action, He commanded His disciples to do as He did. 'Jesus . . . saw a man named Matthew sitting at the receipt of custom, and He saith unto him, Follow Me.' He did not dismiss His followers as pupils to a task, He declared that they would have a common life with Him. ' Verily, verily, I say unto you, I am the door of the sheep . . . by Me, if any man enter in, He shall be saved, and shall go in and out and find pasture.' Jesus combines every side of religion in Himself, and is the sum of His Gospel. ' I am the way, the truth, and the life.'

Jesus made a claim that separates Him from every other teacher—a claim of solitary and absolute infallibility. The attitude of other masters has been modest and qualified. 'This, I think, is true, but you must not believe it as my word; this, I think, is right, but you must not do it after my example. Examine and decide for yourselves. I am, like yourselves, a seeker and a sinner.' Their disciples accepted this situation, and so Simmias said to Socrates, 'We must learn, or we must discover for ourselves, the truth of these matters; or if that be impossible, we must take the best and most impregnable of human doctrines, and, embarking on that as on a raft, risk the voyage of life, unless a stronger vessel, some divine word, could be found on which we might take our journey more safely and more securely. . . . Cebes and I have been considering your argument, and we think that it is barely sufficient.'

'I daresay you are right, my friend,' said Socrates in the *Phaedo*.

Jesus did not affect such humility, nor make such admissions. He did not obliterate or minimise Himself; He emphasised and asserted Himself. 'Ye have heard that it hath been said by them of old time,' opens one paragraph after another of Jesus' great sermon, and then follows, 'But I say unto you.' Jesus brushes aside the ancients as if they had never been. His disciples were not to own any authority beside Him ; He was to be absolute, with Apostles and Prophets only His witnesses and interpreters, never His equals. 'Be not ye called Rabbi, for One is your master, even Christ, and all ye are brethren.' His words are ushered in with the solemn formula, 'Verily, verily' ; they fall on the inner ear like the stroke of a bell ; they are independent of argument. It is ever 'I,' and one's soul answers with reverence. Fort his 'I' that sounds from every sentence of the teaching of Jesus is not egotism ; it is Deity.

Jesus makes the most unqualified demand on the loyalty of His disciples, and believes that the attraction of His Person will sustain their obedience. The beginning of the religious life was no reception of dogma or dream of mysticism ; it was to break up a man's former environment, and to follow the lead of Christ. 'Believe in Me,' and 'Come to Me,' He was ever saying, as if it were natural to trust Him, impossible to resist Him. The hardness of religion had its compensations : it carried association with Jesus. 'Whosoever will come after Me, let him deny himself, and take up his cross and follow Me.' The immense sacrifices of religion would be an office of love. 'There is no man that hath left house, or brethren, or sisters, or father, or mother, or wife, or children, or lands, for my sake.' . . . Religious cowardice was a synonym for treachery to Christ; it was a breach of friendship that could not be healed. 'Whosoever shall be ashamed of Me and of My words, of him shall the Son of Man be ashamed when He shall come in His own glory, and in His Father's, and of the holy angels.' The slightest kindness was exalted into an act of merit, because it was inspired by devotion to Christ. 'For whosoever shall give you a cup of water to drink in My name, because ye belong to Christ, verily I say unto you, he shall not lose his reward.' When Jesus came from the Father, the religious instincts were withering in the dust, and vainly feeling for something on which they could climb to God; Jesus presented Himself, and gathered the tendrils of the soul round His Person. He found religion a rite; He left it a passion.

Perhaps the most brilliant inspiration of

Jesus was to fling Himself on the earliest, latest, strongest passion of our nature, and utilise it as the driving force of His religion. All our life from infancy to age we are in the school of love, and never does human nature so completely shed the slough of selfishness, or wear so generous a guise, or offer such ungrudging service as when under this sway. Here is stored to hand the latent dynamic for a spiritual enterprise; it only remains to make the connection. Do you wish a cause to endure hardness, to rejoice in sacrifice, to accomplish mighty works, to retain for ever the dew of its youth? Give it the best chance, the sanction of Love. Do not state it in books; do not defend it with argument. These are aids of the second order; if they succeed, it is a barren victory—the reason only has been won; if they fail, it is a hopeless defeat—the reason has now been exasperated. Identify your cause with a person. Even a bad cause will succeed for a space, associated with an attractive man. The later Stewarts were hard kings both to England and Scotland, and yet women sent their husbands and sons to die for 'Bonnie Prince Charlie,' and the ashes of

that romantic devotion are not yet cold.
When a good cause finds a befitting leader, it
will be victorious before set of sun. David
had about him such a grace of beauty and
chivalry that his officers risked their lives
to bring him a cup of water, and his people
carried him to the throne of Israel on the love
of their hearts. Human nature has two dominant instincts—the spring of all action as well
as the subject of all literature—Faith and
Love. The religion which unites them will be
omnipotent.

It was Jesus who summoned Love to meet
the severe demands of Faith, and wedded for
the first time the ideas of Passion and Righteousness. Hitherto Righteousness had been
spotless and admirable, but cold as ice; Passion had been sweet and strong, but unchast-
ened and wanton. Jesus suddenly identifies
Righteousness with Himself, and has brought
it to pass that no man can love Him without
loving Righteousness. Jesus clothes Himself
with the commandments, and each is trans-
figured into a grace. He illustrates His Dec-
alogue in the washing of feet, and compels
His disciples to follow His example. 'If I

then, your Lord and Master, have washed your
feet, ye ought also to wash one another's feet.'
By one felicitous stroke He makes Love and
Law synonymous, and Duty, which had always
been respectable, now becomes lovely. It is a
person, not a dogma, which invites my faith;
a person, not a code, which asks for obedience.
Jesus stands in the way of every selfishness;
He leads in the path of every sacrifice; He is
crucified in every act of sin; He is glorified in
every act of holiness. St. Stephen, as he suffered for the Gospel, saw the heavens open and
Jesus standing to receive him. St. Peter fleeing in a second panic from Rome, meets Jesus
returning to be crucified in his place. Conscience and heart are settled on Jesus, and one
feels within his soul the tides of His virtue.
It is not the doctrines nor the ethics of Christianity that are its irresistible attraction. Its
doctrines have often been a stumbling-block,
and its ethics excel only in degree. The life
blood of Christianity is Christ. As Louis said
'L'état c'est moi,' so may Jesus say ' I am My
Religion.' What Napoleon was to his soldiers
on the battle-field, Jesus has been to millions
separated from Him by the chasm of centuries.

No emotion in human experience has been so masterful, none so fruitful, as the passion for Jesus.   It has inspired the Church, it has half saved the world.

Before Jesus could utilise this love   He had to create it, and this was not accomplished either by His example or His teaching.   The effect of His awful purity was terror : ' Depart from me,' said St. Peter, ' for I am a sinful man, O Lord.'   The result of three years' teaching was perplexity : an average apostle asked for a theophany :   ' Show us the Father, and it sufficeth us.'   Holiness compels awe, wisdom compels respect; they do not allure.   Nothing can create Life but Life; nothing can beget Love but Love.   He that is not loved hates; he that is loved, loves, is a law of experience.   As the earth gives out the heat which it has received from the sun, so the devotion of Jesus' disciples to Him in all ages has been the return of His immense devotion to them.   He lavished on His first disciples a wealth of love in His friendship; He sealed it with His sacrifice of Himself upon the cross.   ' Greater love hath no man than this, that a man lay down his life for his friends.'   ' I am the good Shepherd :

the good Shepherd giveth His life for the sheep.'
Twelve men came into His intimacy; in eleven
he kindled a fire that made them saints and
heroes, and the traitor broke his heart through
remorse, so he also must have loved.   But Jesus
expected that His love would have a wider
range than the fellowship of Galilee, and that
the world would yield to its spell.   It was not
for St. John, His friend, Jesus laid down His
life; it was for the Race into which He had
been born and which He carried in His heart.
No one has ever made such a sacrifice for
Humanity.   No one has dared to ask such a
recompense.   The eternal Son of God gave
Himself without reserve, and anticipated that
to all time men would give themselves for Him.
He proposed to inspire His Race with a personal devotion, and that profound devotion was
to be their salvation.   'Give Me a cross where-
on to die,' said Jesus, ' and I will make thereof
a throne from which to rule the world.'   The
idea was once at least caught most perfectly in
an early Christian gem, where, on a blood-red
stone the living Christ is carved against His
cross; a Christ with the insignia of His imperial
majesty.   Twice was Jesus' imagination power-

fully affected—once by the horrors of the cross, when He prayed, ' O My Father, if it be possible, let this cup pass from Me '; that was the travail of His soul—once by the magnetic attraction of the cross, when He cried, ' And I, if I be lifted up from the earth, will draw all men unto Me '; this is the endless reward of His travail.

The passion for Jesus has no analogy in comparative religion; it has no parallel in human experience. It is a flame of unique purity and intensity. Thomas does not believe that Jesus is the Son of God, or that, more than any other man, He can escape the hatred of fanaticism; but he must share the fate of Jesus. ' Let us also go,' said this morbid sceptic, ' that we may die with Him.' At the sight of His face seven devils went out of Mary Magdalene; for the blessing of His visit, a chief publican gave half his goods to the poor. When a man of the highest order met Jesus he was lifted into the heavenly places and became a Christed man, whose eyes saw with the vision of Christ, whose pulse beat with the heart of Christ. Browning has nothing finer than 'A Death in the Desert,' wherein he imagines the love of St. John to

Jesus.   No power is able to rouse the apostle
from his last sleep, neither words nor cordials.
Then one has a sudden inspiration : he brings
the Gospel and reads into the unconscious ear,

'I am the resurrection and the life,'

with the effect of an instantaneous charm.

'Whereat he opened his eyes wide at once
And sat up of himself and looked at us.'

This man had leant so long on Jesus' bosom
—some seventy years—that at the very sound
of His words the soul of Jesus' friend came up
from the shadow of death.   It is the response
of the flower of the Race to Jesus.

This passion is placed beyond comparison,
because it is independent of sight.   St. Paul
denied the faith that was once dear to him, and
flung away the world that was once his ambition, to welcome innumerable labours and ex-
haust the resources of martyrdom, for the sake
of one whom he had never seen, save in mystical
vision, and formerly hated to the shedding of
blood.   Men were lit as torches in Nero's garden, and women flung to the wild beasts of the
amphitheatre ; and for what?   For a system,
for a cause, for a Church?   They had not

enough knowledge of theory to pass a Sunday-school examination; they had no doctrine of the Holy Trinity, nor of the Person of Jesus, nor of His Sacrifice, nor of Grace. They died in their simplicity for Him 'Whom having not seen ye love,' and the name of the Crucified was the last word that trembled on their dying lips. With an amazing candour Jesus had warned His disciples: 'Ye shall be brought before governors and kings for My sake. . . . And ye shall be hated of all men for My name's sake.' With a magnificent confidence Jesus encouraged His disciples, 'He that endureth to the end shall be saved. . . . Whosoever therefore shall confess Me before men, him will I confess also before My Father which is in Heaven.' The warning and the promise were both fulfilled in the history of the disciples' passion. 'Christianus sum,' confesses the martyr, and then the hoarse refrain 'Christianus ad leonem.' But Perpetua sees a 'great ladder of gold reaching from earth to heaven,' and on its highest round stands the Good Shepherd; while Saturus is brought to the throne of the Lord Jesus and 'gathered to His embrace.' 'Men,' says Mr. Lecky, 'seemed indeed to be in love

N

with death. Believing they were the wheat of God, they panted for the day when they should be ground by the teeth of wild beasts into the pure bread of Christ.' Love of life and love of kin, fear of pain and fear of death, were powerless before this talisman ' For My sake.'

This sublime passion did not die with the sacrifice of the martyrs, a mere hysteric of Religion, for it has continued unto this day the hidden spring of all sacrifice and beauty in the Christian life. The immense superstitions of the Middle Ages were redeemed by the love of Jesus, radiant in the life of St. Francis, reflected from the labours of the 'Friends of God.' There was a glory over all the bitter controversies of the sixteenth century, because on the one side piety desired a spiritual access to Jesus' Person; and on the other, piety longed for the comfort of His Real Presence. Both the excessive ceremonialism and the vulgar sensationalism, which are the two poles of modern religion, may be pardoned, because the High Churchman at his altar and the evangelist at the street corner are one in their utter devotion to Jesus. Not only has the best theology been fed by this spirit, so that Bonaventura, questioned regarding his learning, pointed to the crucifix; and the living hymnology been its incarnation, so that to remove the name of Jesus were to leave no fragrance ; but all the vast and varied philanthropy of public Christianity and the sweet and winsome graces of private life have been the fruit of this unworldly emotion. 'For My sake,' has opened a new spring of conduct, from which has flowed the heroism and saintliness of nineteen centuries. When Jesus founded His religion on personal attachment, it seemed a fond imagination: the perennial vitality of Christianity has been His vindication.

This perpetual passion in the hearts of His disciples implies the mystical presence of Jesus, who promised, 'A little while and ye shall not see Me, and again a little while and ye shall see Me, because I go to the Father,' and 'Lo, I am with you alway, even unto the end of the world.' The presence of the living Christ, the object of adoration and service, has been wonderfully realised by the mystics, and distinctly held forth in the sacraments, but it is apt to be obscured in the consciousness of the Church by two different influences. One is a mechanical theology which builds every act of Christ into the structure of a system till no virtue comes from the flowing garments of His life, because they are nothing but the grave-clothes of a dead Lord. The other is an idealising criticism, which evaporates the Person of Christ in His teaching, and while it may leave us a master, certainly denies us a Lord. This were to cast Religion back on its former condition when it was either an invention of the scribes or the philosophers, and to barter the indescribable charm of Christianity to secure a creed or to disarm unbelief. It is to reduce the religion of Jesus to the impotence of Judaism or Confucianism: it is to sell Jesus again without the thirty pieces of silver.

Jesus' idea lifts Christianity above the plane of arid discussion and places it in the region of poetry, where the emotions have full play and Faith is vision. Theology becomes the explanation of the fellowship between the soul and Jesus. Regeneration is the entrance into His life, Justification the partaking of His Cross, Sanctification the transformation into His character, Death the coming of the Lord, Heaven His unveiled Face. Doctrines will be but

moods of the Christ-consciousness; parables of
the Christ-life. Suffering will be the baptism of
Jesus and the drinking of His cup, and if every
saint have not the stigmata on his hands and
feet, he will at least, like Simon the Cyrenian,
have the mark of the Cross upon his shoulder.
And service will be the personal tribute to
Jesus, whom we shall recognise under any disguise, as his nurse detected Ulysses by his
wounds, and whose Body, in the poor and
miserable, will ever be with us for our dis-
discernment. Jesus is the leper whom the saint
kissed, and the child the monk carried over the
stream, and the sick man the widow nursed into
health, after the legends of the ages of faith.
And Jesus will say at the close of the day,
'Inasmuch as ye have done it unto one of the
least of these my brethren ye have done it
unto Me.'

We ought to discern the real strength of
Christianity and revive the ancient passion for
Jesus. It is the distinction of our religion: it
is the guarantee of its triumph. Faith may
languish; creeds may be changed; churches
may be dissolved; society may be shattered.
But one cannot imagine the time when Jesus

will not be the fair image of perfection, or the circumstances wherein He will not be loved. He can never be superseded; he can never be exceeded. Religions will come and go, the passing shapes of an eternal instinct, but Jesus will remain the standard of the conscience and the satisfaction of the heart, Whom all men seek, in Whom all men will yet meet.

198   THE MIND OF THE MASTER

JUDGMENT ACCORDING TO TYPE

X

JUDGMENT ACCORDING TO TYPE

Two at least of the chief convictions which sustain the heart of Humanity rest, in the last issue, on a basis of pure reason. One is the belief that the soul is immortal; the other is the belief that it will be judged. We repudiate the opposite, because the annihilation of the spiritual and the confusion of the moral are unthinkable. 'For my own part,' says Mr. Fiske, 'I believe in the immortality of the soul, not in the sense in which I accept the demonstrable truths of science, but as a supreme act of faith in the reasonableness of God's work.' It is incredible that when the long evolution of nature has come to a head the flower should be flung away. This were to reduce design to a fiasco. 'What can be more in the essential nature of things,' writes Mr. W. R. Greg, in his *Enigmas of Life*, a very honest book, 'than that the mere entrance into the spiritual state will effect a severance of souls?' It is incredible that the present failure of justice should end in no redress, and the immense wrongs of this life have no 'complement of recompense.' This were to turn order to chaos, and put us all to 'permanent intellectual confusion.' Pessimistic thinkers, whose reason has been deflected by the presence of an arrogant materialism, and moral triflers, whose conscience is satisfied with a deity of imbecile good nature—the *bon Dieu* of the French—may deny jndgment; the one, because there is no soul, the other, because there is no judge. But the masters of thought in all ages and of all nations have accepted judgment as an axiom in the calculation of human life; they have used it as a factor in the creation of human history. Reference of every moral action to an eternal standard, revisal of every individual life by a supreme authority, are embedded in the creeds of the Race. The *Book of the Dead* was the sacred writing of the oldest civilisation, and it describes how the soul is weighed in the intangible scales of righteousness. The Greek moralists conceived the

Furies let loose on the guilty soul, and placed their abode behind the judgment seat of Areopagus. The 'Bible of the Middle Ages' was a rehearsal of judgment, wherein not only the saints and sinners of the past, but those of that very day, received their due recompense of reward. Angelico wrought out his Inferno and Paradiso in a picture which fails somewhat on the left hand, where sinners are tormented by their own sins, because he was ignorant of sin, but succeeds gloriously on the right, where the glorified arrive in a flower-garden—which is the outer court of Heaven—for he only of men had seen the angels. When the ages of faith had closed and every conviction of the past was put to the question, one belief still held an iron grip, and Michael Angelo painted his Judgment in the Pope's Chapel of the Vatican. It is a picture which confuses and overwhelms one; it was an awful agony of Art · but it was also an intense reality of the soul.

We have a robust common sense of morality which refuses to believe that it does not matter whether a man has lived like the Apostle Paul or the Emperor Nero. One may hesitate to speculate about the circumstances of the other world; one may love the splendid imagination of the Apocalypse more than the vulgar realism of modern sentiment, but one can never crush out the conviction that there must be one place for St. John, who was Jesus' friend, and another for Judas Iscariot, who was His betrayer. It were unreasonable that this mad confusion of circumstances should continue, which ties up the saint and the miscreant together to the misery of both; it were supremely reasonable that this tangle be unravelled and each receive his satisfaction. One has seen sheep and swine feeding in the same field till evening, and has followed till the sheep were gathered into their fold, and the swine ran greedily to their stye. The last complaint that would have occurred to one's mind was that their owners had separated them, the last suggestion that they should be herded together. What was fitting had happened; it was separation according to type.

Jesus did not supersede this conviction as the superstition of an imperfect morality, nor condemn it as a contradiction of the Divine Love. His 'enthusiasm of Humanity' did not blind Him to deep lines of moral demarcation;

His 'huge tenderness' did not propose an equality for Judas and John. He did not come to reduce the moral order to an anarchy of grace, and to break the inevitable connection between sin and punishment. It has been said by a profound thinker that Antinomianism is the only heresy, and it is desirable to remind one's self, in a day of flabby sentiment, that Jesus was not an Antinomian. Had Jesus condoned sin, then He had been the destroyer of our Race, and not its Saviour, for the comforting of our heart had been a poor recompense for the debauchery of our conscience. But it is a conspicuous instance of Jesus' balance, that He combined the most tender compassion for the sinner with the most unflinching condemnation of sin. It is Jesus who has compared sin unto Gehenna, 'where their worm dieth not and the fire is not quenched'; who places the rich man of soft and luxurious life in torment, so that he begs for a drop of water to cool his tongue; who casts the unprofitable servant into outer darkness, where is weeping and gnashing of teeth; who declares that the fruitless branches of the vine will be gathered and burned; who sends the servants of self into the fire prepared for the Devil and his angels. Jesus spake in parables, and it were folly to press His words into a description of circumstances. Jesus spake also with marked emphasis, and it were dishonesty to deny that He believed in the fact of judgment.

Jesus went with the general reason of the Race in affirming the certainty of judgment, and therein He is at one with the Catholic creeds of Christendom. Jesus has also gone with the general reason in affirming the morality of judgment, and therein He has differed from that solitary creed which has raised uncharitableness into an article of faith. What has filled many honourable minds with resentment and rebellion is not the fact of separation, but the principle of execution; not the dislike of an assortment, but the fear that it will not be into good and bad. No power will ever convince a reasonable being that one man should be elected to life and have Heaven settled on him as an entailed estate, and another be ordained to death and 'be held in the way thereto'; or that one be 'blessed' because he has held the orthodox creed, and another be 'cursed' be-

cause he has made a mistake in the most profound of all sciences. If Heaven and Hell—
be they places or states—are made to hinge on
the arbitrary will of the Almighty, or on the
imperfect processes of human reason, then
Judgment will not be a fiasco, it will be an
outrage. It will be a climax of irresponsible
despotism, whose monstrous injustice would
leave Heaven without blessing and Hell without curse.

Reason cannot agree with such a reading of
judgment ; reason cannot disagree with the
reading of Jesus. Jesus never made judgment
depend either on the will of God or the belief
of man. He rested judgment on the firm foundation of what each man is in the sight of the
Eternal. He anticipated no protest in his parables against the justice of this evidence : none
has ever been made from any quarter. The
wheat is gathered into the garner. What else
could one do with wheat ? The tares are burned
in the fire. What else could one do with tares ?
When the net comes to the shore, the good fish
are gathered into vessels ; no one would throw
them away. The bad are cast aside ; no one
would leave them to contaminate the good.

The supercilious guests who did not value the great supper were left severely alone. If men do not care for Heaven, they will not be forced into it. The outcasts, who had never dared to dream of such a supper, were compelled to come. If men hunger for the best, the best shall be theirs. The virgins who had taken the trouble of bringing oil went in to the marriage ; they were evidently friends of the bridegroom : the virgins who had made no preparation were shut out from the marriage ; they were mere strangers. Had the foolish virgins been rejected because they were a few minutes late, they would have had just cause of complaint. When the bridegroom declined their company for the simple reason that He did not know them, they had no answer. It would be equally out of place either for friends to be refused, or strangers to force admission to a marriage. It is all fair and fitting—exactly as things ought to be : Jesus' judgment is the very apotheosis of reason.

Twice has the Judgment been described with authority—once by the greatest prophet that has spoken outside the Hebrew succession, once by the chief prophet of Jew and Gentile.

Plato has told us that the judges of the great assizes will sit at a place on the other side, where all roads from this world meet, and where, divided by the throne of justice, they part again into two—the way which leadeth to the Islands of the Blessed, and the way that goeth to the 'House of Vengeance and Punishment, which is called Tartarus.' Men are not to appear before the judges in the body, lest justice should be partial, since there are many 'having evil souls who are apparelled in fair bodies': neither are the judges to be clothed, lest their bodies be 'interposed as a veil before their own souls.' The judgment is to be absolutely real; each judge 'with his naked soul shall pierce into the other naked soul,' and each soul will go to its own place. Just as bodies have a shape of their own, so is it with souls. Some are scarred by crimes, some are crooked with falsehood, some deformed by incontinence; these are despatched to Tartarus. Other souls show the fair proportions of holiness and truth, and on them the judges look with admiration as they go to the Islands of the Blessed. Nothing is arbitrary; everything is reasonable. It is registration rather than examination; it is fulfilment rather than judgment.

The Judgment of Plato is one of the supreme efforts of human reason, surely not unilluminated by the Spirit of God; and one compares it with the Judgment of Jesus to find a considerable difference in drapery, and an exact correspondence in principle. According to Jesus, there will be a Judgment on the confines of the 'Unseen Universe,' and each soul will appear before Him seated on the Throne of His glory. There will be instant division, but no confusion: it will be manifestation and confirmation. The sheep and the goats, which have been one flock in the pastures of this life, will fall apart, each breed according to its nature. Those who have lived the selfless life, who saw Him an hungered and gave Him meat, fulfilling the Law of Love, shall stand on one side, because by their choice they are of one kind; and those who have loved the self life, who saw Him a stranger and took Him not in, disobeying the Law of Love, shall stand on the other side, because by their choice they are of another kind. 'Come, ye blessed' is said to the selfless, because by the constitution of the moral universe they cannot be anything else than blessed. 'Depart, ye cursed' is said to the selfish because even God Himself could not prevent them being cursed. Their state in neither case is 'prepared,' but is the inheritance of character. It is a recognition of fitness, as reasonable as an arrangement into species, as natural as the ripening of harvest.

Jesus makes a marked advance on Plato by magnifying the function of the Judge, and anticipating the date of the Judgment. The Judge in St. Matthew's Gospel is not an official referring to a Law: He is identical with the Law itself. Each soul is tried not by its obedience to a written standard, but by its relation to a living Person. Jesus' 'Come' is the symbol of a Law, the Law of attraction. His 'Depart' is the symbol of another Law, the Law of repulsion, and Jesus Himself is in both events the magnetic force. The personal factor, which is the heart of the religion of Jesus, asserts itself in the Judgment. Jesus monopolises the outlook of life: He is the wounded Man the priest passes, whom the Samaritan helps. His acceptance or rejection is the test of the soul, and the crisis simply culminates at the Judgment. Human life will then finally break against Jesus as a rock in the midst of a stream, each current to follow its own direction unfettered and unmingled. The presence of Jesus is our Judgment.

We are accustomed to refer Judgment to the threshold of the other world. We ought to acclimatise the idea in this world, for if Jesus once enlarged on the august circumstances of the future Judgment, He referred continually to the awful responsibility of a present Judgment. One can easily understand how the revelation of Jesus' moral Glory on the other side will raise to the highest power both His attraction and His repulsion, and suddenly crystallise into permanence the fluid principles of a man's life. The stream will be frozen in the fall. But this will only be the consummation of a process which is now in action. Jesus has not to wait for His Throne to command attention or affect the soul. He is the most dominant and exacting Personality in human experience, from whose magical circle of influence none can tear himself. Can any one follow Jesus' life from Nazareth to Calvary, and stand face to face with Jesus' Cross, and be neither

better nor worse? Incredible and impossible.
Certain minds may hesitate over the Nicene
Creed, but it is trifling to treat Jesus as a name
in history, or a character in a book. He is the
Man whom Plato once imagined, whom Isaiah
prophesied, whom the most spiritual desire, who
exhausts Grace and Truth. Beyond all question, and apart from all theories, Jesus is the
Revelation of the Divine goodness: the incarnate Law of God: the objective conscience of
Humanity. As soon as we enter the presence
of Jesus we lose the liberty of moral indifference. One Person we cannot avoid—the inevitable Christ; one dilemma we must face,
'What shall I do with Jesus which is called
Christ.' The spiritual majesty of this Man
arraigns us at His bar from which we cannot
depart till we become His disciples or His
critics, His friends or His enemies. With certain consequences. Belief in Jesus is justification, for it is loyalty to the best; disbelief in
Jesus is condemnation, it is enmity to the best.
Jesus stated the position in a classical passage,
'He that believeth on Him is not condemned:
but he that believeth not is condemned already,
because he hath not believed in the name of

the only begotten Son of God. And this is
the condemnation, that light is come into the
world, and men loved darkness rather than
light, because their deeds were evil.'

As the mere presence of a good man in a
room will compel the silent opinion of every
other person, and be their judgment, so Jesus
was for three years, from His public appearance
at Nazareth to His crucifixion on Calvary, a
criterion of character and a factor of division.
He was the problem burdening every man's
intellect, the law stimulating every man's conscience, the life exciting every man's imagination, the figure by which all kinds of men ad-
justed themselves. According to the Gospels,
every one was sensitive to Jesus. As soon as
He was born wise men came from far to worship Him, and Herod sent soldiers to slay Him.
When He was presented in the Temple, Simeon
took the infant in his arms and spake by the
Holy Ghost, 'Behold, this child is set for the
fall and rising again of many in Israel.' If He
preached in the synagogue of His boyhood, the
people, under the irresistible influence of Jesus'
Personality, 'wondered at the gracious word
which proceeded out of His mouth,' so strong

was His power of attraction, and then would have 'cast Him down headlong,' so great was His power of repulsion. If He visited a country town in Galilee, a Pharisee would invite Him to a feast in order to insult Him, and a publican would make a 'great feast in his own house,' in order to honour Him. The people were divided over Jesus, 'for some said, He is a good Man,' others said, Nay, but He deceiveth the people, and the very Council was torn with controversy, the majority sending officers to arrest Him, but Nicodemus breaking silence in His defence. If two men disputed in those days, it was about Jesus; if they talked together by the way, it was of Jesus; the atmosphere was electrical with Jesus. 'Whom do men say that I, the Son of Man, am?' asked Jesus of His disciples, for He knew they could not ignore Him. It was a day of judgment—searching and conclusive. To so many Jesus was the 'Son of the living God,' to so many, 'a man gluttonous and a winebibber, a friend of publicans and sinners.' He was either the Rock on which wise men built, or the stone which would grind wicked men to powder. Jesus was much impressed by the

spectacle of this unconscious but decisive judgment. 'The Father judgeth no man, but hath
committed all judgment unto the Son. . . .
Verily, verily, I say unto you, the hour is coming, and now is, when the dead shall hear the
voice of the Son of God, and they that hear
shall live. . . . And (the Father) hath given
Him authority to execute judgment also, because He is the Son of Man.'

Jesus compared Himself to the Light because it bringeth to the birth everything that is
good in the world, and as Jesus fulfilled His
course, elect souls were drawn to Him. Simeon
saw Him only in His weakness, and was ready
to 'depart in peace'; John Baptist recognised
Him of a sudden, and laid down his ministry
at Jesus' feet; St. John spent one night with
Him, and followed Him unto old age; St.
Matthew heard one word from Him, and left
all he had; a dying robber had the good fortune to be crucified beside Him, and acknowledged Him King of Paradise. There was a
latent affinity between these men and Jesus.
He was the Good Shepherd, and they were
'His own sheep.' 'He calleth His own sheep
by name . . . and the sheep follow Him.'

Jesus also compared Himself to Light because it layeth bare every evil thing, and the light of Jesus raised sin to its height. The Sadducean priests accomplished His crucifixion, lest He should diminish their Temple gains; the Pharisees hated Him to death because He had exposed their hypocrisy; the foolish people turned against Him because He would not feed them with bread; Herod Antipas set Him at nought because Jesus did not play the conjuror for his amusement; Pilate sent Jesus to the cross in order to save his office; Judas Iscariot betrayed Him because he could now make no other gain of Him. There was a latent antipathy between these men and Jesus. 'If God were your Father,' Jesus said to such men once, 'ye would love Me: for I proceeded forth and came from God. . . . Ye are of your father the devil, and the lusts of your father ye will do.'

It was a drama of judgments, conducted in the face of the world for three years, with an evident justification and an evident condemnation, but the former did not of necessity imply a visible goodness, nor the latter a visible badness on the part of the judged. Those who approximated to the John type were not at all saintly: St. Matthew was a publican, and St. Mary Magdalene was a sinner. There was simply one point in their favour, they hated their evil selves and welcomed Jesus' cross. Those who approximated to the Judas type were not all evil livers. The Pharisees were careful about the works of the Law, and devoted to the cause of Judaism. There was only one point against them, they were satisfied with themselves, and were determined to have nothing to do with Jesus' cross. The children of Light are not so much those who have walked in the Light as those who love the Light. The children of darkness are not so much those who walked in darkness as those who love darkness. There were men ready for Jesus because they had 'an honest and good heart.' There were men alien to Jesus because they were sensual and hyprocrites. It is a question not so much of action as of bias.

Jesus knew that it was not possible to divide men into two classes by the foliage of the outer life, as it is seen from the highway. Few people are saints or devils in their daily conduct: most are a mixture of good and bad. Below the variety of action lies the unity of principle. Some people have grave faults and yet we believe they are good; some are paragons of respectability and yet we are sure they are bad. No one would refuse St. Peter a place with Jesus, although he denied Him once with curses; none propose a place with Jesus for Judas although he only committed himself once in public. An instinct tells us the direction of the soul; the trend of character. We concur with the judgment of Jesus, Who said of Judas, 'One of you is a devil'; but of St. Peter, 'Satan hath desired to have you, that he may sift you as wheat, but I have prayed for thee.'

When Jesus judges by type, our Christ approximation, or our Christ alienation, one is struck by His absolute fairness. We are estimated not by what we have done but by what we desire to be. With Jesus the purpose of the soul is as the soul's achievement, and He will not be disappointed. If one surrender himself to Jesus, and is crucified on His cross, there is no sin he will not overcome, no service he will not render, no virtue to which he will not attain. He has made a good beginning, he has a long time. If one refuse the appeal of Jesus, and cling to his lower self, there is no degradation to which he may not descend. He has made a bad beginning, and he also has a long time. Both have eternity. We choose our type, and with God it is fulfilled; so that St. Mary Magdalene in her penitence was saved, and Simon in his self-righteousness lost already.

'All instincts immature,
  All purposes unsure,
  That weighed not as his work, yet swelled the man's
    account;
  Thoughts hardly to be packed
  Into a narrow act,
  Fancies that broke through language and escaped;
  All I could never be,
  All men ignored in me,
  This I was worth to God whose wheel the pitcher shaped.'

Judgment by type sets the future in a new and solemn light. We can no longer think of Heaven as a state of certain happiness, and Hell as a state of certain misery, for every man, whatever may be his ideal. They are now relative terms, so that one man's Heaven might be another man's Hell. If one hunger and thirst for God, then for him is prepared the beatific vision and the eternal service. He has his heaven, and is satisfied. If one seek nothing beyond himself and his own gratification, then he will be left to himself, and taste the fulness of his lusts. He has his hell and is satisfied. St. John was already in Heaven with his head on Jesus' bosom. Judas was in Hell as he went into the outer darkness. Each was at home, the one with Jesus, the other away from Jesus. None need be afraid that he who has followed Jesus will miss heaven, or that he who has made the 'great refusal' will be thrust into Heaven. One is afraid that some will inherit Hell and be content.

OPTIMISM THE ATTITUDE OF FAITH

XI

OPTIMISM THE ATTITUDE OF FAITH

Professor Orr opens his admirable Kerr Lectures on the 'Christian View of God and the World,' with an exposition of the German idea, 'Weltansicht,' and pleads with much force for a Christian theory of the world. It is an interesting coincidence that the two eminent men who delivered the last Gifford Lectures have both addressed themselves to the same subject in their treatment of religion. The Master of Balliol, in his *Evolution of Religion*, and Professor Pfleiderer, in his *Philosophy of Religion*, have felt it necessary to embrace 'Optimism and Pessimism.' It is a sign of the times : it is also a reflection on the past. Philosophy for more than a century has realised the situation, and has faced the problem of the Race with energy and tenacity. 'What is the meaning of Life?' and 'What is its drift?' this kind of question lay heavy on the mind of thinkers, and they did their best to answer it. Unfortunately the apparatus at their command was defective, for the philosophers were not able to avail themselves of the two chief factors in the situation—the revelation of the Will of God in sacred history, and the Incarnation of our Lord Jesus Christ. They worked with the postulates of reason and the visible facts of history. Sometimes they came to a conclusion of hope, sometimes of despair : but they wrestled to the end with unshaken courage. Whether philosophy has failed or succeeded, it deserves the credit of an honourable attempt. Philosophy was not blind to the world out-look, nor indifferent to the world-sorrow.

While the problem has taken shape within a century, it has existed since the beginning of ordered thought, and the pendulum has swung with regular beat between two extremes. The Homeric age with its frank joy in nature—the brightness of the sky and the glory of a man's strength—which is the fresh youth of the world—was followed by the age of Æschylus with its sense of the tragedy of life—its shameful falls, its irresistible hindrances, its inevitable woes—

which is the haggard manhood of the world. The splendid idealism of the greater Hebrew prophets who saw the dawn breaking afar on the Person of the Messiah gave way to the bitter cynicism of the author of Ecclesiastes. Judaism, if you accept the Prophets as its most characteristic interpreters, raised optimism to a creed and embodied it as a people. Buddhism, if you judge it by the example of its illustrious founder, disparaged even existence, and has clouded the horizon of the East. At the beginning of last century Leibnitz declared this the best of all possible worlds, and towards its close Rousseau preached a state of nature as Paradise, but after this century had been born in blood and fire, Schopenhauer considered that life was less than gain, and Leopardi hungered for death. In our own day we have heard Emerson lift up his voice in perpetual sunshine, and have gone with Carlyle when he walked in darkness and saw no light; and if Pippa sings,—

> ' God's in His heaven,
> All's right with the world,'

Thompson has written the 'City of Dreadful

Night.' It is a long action and reaction—an antithesis that, outside Religion, has no synthesis, and one is driven to the conclusion that optimism and pessimism are only half truths. They are the offspring of moods of thought, and carried to an extreme include their own Nemesis. The shallow optimism of Leibnitz was the preparation for Schopenhauer, and the morbid pessimism of Hartmann is a prophecy of optimism.

The controversies of philosophy have often been metaphysical—in the regions beyond life, but no one can deny that this long strife has been practical—in the midst of life's hurly-burly. No human being can escape it unless he be dead to the passion of Humanity, or unless he had never realised the distinction between what is and what ought to be—the Real and the Ideal. The unspeakable agony of human life, which has been a long Gethsemane, and the unintelligible condition of the lower animals, which is a very carnival of slaughter, beat on the doors of reason and heart. It is not wonderful that some have tried to shelter themselves in a fool's Paradise from the groans they could not still, or that others, feeling the hideous facts, judged

is better to die than to live,—that some have
imagined no other God than a blind and cruel
Necessity, or that others have conceived two
contending forces of good and evil. Nothing
is wonderful in speculation or action save indifference to the enigma of life.

One recognises the limitations of Philosophy,
and turns with expectation to Theology, which
is fully equipped for the solution of this problem. Theology is the science of religion,
whose work it is to collect and analyse the facts
of the spiritual consciousness, and it is rich in
treasures. It has, for instance, a doctrine of
God, with profound conceptions of His righteousness and love, His wisdom and power.
Correlate the character of God and the destiny
of the Race. Should not this illuminate the
darkness? Theology has a doctrine of the Incarnation, which implies the union of humanity
with Himself in the Eternal Son of God. Is
this high alliance to have no influence on the
future of the Race? Theology has also a
doctrine of the Holy Ghost, which asserts the
Presence of God in this world and His continual operation. Will not the immanence of
God carry great issues? From her standpoint

Theology commands the situation in its length and breadth, and can speak with a solitary authority on the mystery of life and the goal of the Race. It suddenly occurs to one as amazing that Philosophy should undertake a subject for which Theology alone can be adequate.

It is much more amazing to discover that on this burning question Theology up till quite a recent date has been silent, and still delays her deliverance. Christian Theology has nothing to say to the Race; her concern has been wholly with the individual. The Race has been the subject of a huge catastrophe, and is left out of account. It is on the individual Theology expends all her labour, and her most elaborate doctrines are the explanation how he is to be saved from the general wreckage. Her outlook for him is an unqualified optimism so far as he is separated from his Race. He will be sustained and trained in this life as in a penitentiary, and then will begin to live in Heaven—his real home. No single doctrine of Theology, with the doubtful exception of original sin, has, till recently, been applied to the Race. The realisation of the Fatherhood, and the expansion of the Incarnation, are of yesterday. Theology will now explore the consequences of the Incarnation, and tell us soon what it means that the Son of God is also the Son of Man. Hitherto pessimism or optimism lay outside Theology because the Race had been abandoned.

When one consults the supreme Book of Religion, the result is at first a perplexity and then an encouragement. Any one might take a brief for the pessimism of the Bible, and prove his case to the hilt. The irresistible assaults of evil, the loathsome taint of sin, the inevitable entail of punishment, the wrong of the innocent, the martyrdom of the righteous, the slavery of labour, the futility of life, the moan of sorrow, are all in this Book, through which the current of human life rushes to the eternal sea. But if one should choose to take a brief for the optimism of the Bible, he could as easily win his case. The beauty of penitence, the passion for God, the struggle after righteousness, the joy of forgiveness, the attainments in character, the examples of patience, the victory over this world, invest human life in the Bible with undying beauty. It is natural that both pessimists and optimists should claim the sanction of the Hebrew Scriptures: that any intelligent reader might lay down the book with the vision of the Race carrying its bitter cross along the Viâ Dolorosa or crowned with glory in the heavenly places. It seems a contradiction: it points to a solution. No one would dare to say that there is no ground for the alternation of moods of hope and despair that have lifted and cast down the seers of our Race. Within one connected and consistent literature both moods find their strongest and sanest utterance—a pessimism that, even in Ecclesiastes, still clings to God and morals, an optimism that is never shallow or material. Within the same book we look for the reconciliation of this long antinomy and the revelation of a deeper unity. We are not disappointed; it is found in Jesus.

No one has seriously denied that Jesus was an optimist, although it has been hinted that He was a dreamer, and no one can object to the optimism of Jesus, for it was in spite of circumstances. He was born of a peasant woman: in early age He worked for His bread: as a Prophet He depended on alms;

during the great three years He knew not where to lay His head. But the bareness and hardship of His life never embittered His soul, neither do they stiffen Him into Stoicism. A sweet contentment possesses Him, and He lives as a child in His Father's house. This poorest of men warns His disciples against carking care and vain anxiety ; He persuades them to a simple faith in the Divine Providence. They are to 'take no thought for the morrow, for the morrow will take thought for the things of itself.' 'Sufficient unto the day is the evil thereof.' They are to 'behold the fowls of the air,' and to 'take no thought for meat or drink,' to 'consider the lilies of the field,' and to 'take no thought for raiment.' Jesus met the grinding poverty of a Galilean peasant's life with one inexhaustible consolation,— 'Your Heavenly Father knoweth that ye have need of all these things.'

The severity of Jesus' circumstances was added to their poverty, since this Man, who lived only for others, was the victim of the most varied injury. He was exiled as soon as He was born ; His townsmen would have killed Him ; His brethren counted Him mad ; the city of His mighty works did not believe; the multitudes He had helped forsook Him; the professional representatives of religion set themselves against Jesus, and pursued this holiest of men with ingenious slanders; He was a 'Samaritan' (or heretic), and 'had a devil'; He was a 'gluttonous man and a winebibber,' and kept disreputable company; He was a blasphemer and deceiver. A huge conspiracy encompassed Him, and laboured for His death; one of His intimates betrayed Him; the priests of God produced false witnesses against Him; the people He loved clamoured for His death; the Roman power He had respected denied Him justice; He was sent to the vilest death. During this long ordeal His serenity was never disturbed; He was never angry save with sin. He never lost control of Himself or became the slave of circumstances. His bequest to the disciples was Peace, and He spake of Joy in the upper room. He was so lifted above the turmoil of this life, that Pilate was amazed; and, amid the agony of the Cross, He prayed for His enemies. Nothing has so embittered men as utter poverty or social injustice. Jesus endured both, and maintained the radiant brightness of His soul.

His was optimism set in the very environment of pessimism.

Jesus saw the Race into which He had been born in the light that illuminated His own life, and held out to them the Hope which sustained His own soul. Pagan poets had placed the age of gold in the far past; Hebrew prophets referred it to the distant future. Jesus dared to say it might be now and here. It was the glory of Isaiah to imagine a Kingdom of Righteousness that would yet be established, with outward sanctions of authority, on earth. It was the achievement of Jesus to set up the Kingdom of Righteousness within the heart with the eternal sanctions of Love. He was the first to insist that the one bondage a man need fear was sin ; that no man need be the slave of sin unless he willed ; that freedom from sin was perfect liberty, and that any man could enter into Heaven by retiring within a clean and loving soul. The highest reaches of optimism have conceived a state of physical comfort and placed it far away. Jesus preached a Kingdom of Holiness, and placed it in the soul. He had the faith to deliver this Gospel where the Jewish world was a hollow unreality, and the Pagan world one corruption. It was the very extravagance of optimism.

The attitude of Jesus was amazing in the wideness of His vision, in the assurance of His hope. His kingdom might be as a grain of mustard seed: in its branches the souls of men would yet take refuge. It might be only a morsel of leaven hidden in the mass of society: the world would be regenerated by its influence. He prepared twelve men with immense care that they might carry His kingdom to the ends of the world. Although He never passed beyond the borders of Syria in His mission, He grasped the nations in His faith, and saw them 'come from the east, and from the west, and from the north, and from the south,' and 'sit down in the Kingdom of God.' Before His betrayal Jesus administered a sacrament that was to last till His second coming. After He rose from the dead He commanded His disciples to evangelise the world. He did not hesitate to say that all men would be drawn to Him, Who was a synonym for Righteousness, Joy and Peace. Jesus hoped the best, not for the individual only, but also for the Race.

The grounds for Jesus' sublime optimism

were three, and the first was the will of God. With the extreme left of pessimism Jesus believed that there was a Will at the heart of the universe working slowly, constantly, and irresistibly. But it is not blind, immoral, impersonal—mere Titanic force. It is the expression and energy of Love. This Will might appear under strange phenomena, might impose great sufferings, might have immense restraint, but it works for goodness. It might send Jesus to the Cross, but now and ever it was a sure and gracious Will. The future lay in that Will and must be bright. It was an ancient Father that said, ' God works all things up into what is better ; ' and a modern heretic who declared, ' God, who spent ages in fitting the earth for the residence of man, may well spend ages more in fitting rectified man to inhabit a renovated earth.' This was the faith and patience of Jesus.

Jesus also believed in man, and therein he differed from the pessimists of His own day. The Pharisees regarded the mass of people as moral refuse, the unavoidable waste from the finished product of Pharisaism. With Jesus the common people were the raw material for the Kingdom of God, rich in the possibilities of sainthood. When Jesus made His own *Apologia* in the 15th chapter of St. Luke's Gospel, He also offered their apology for the people. They were not callous and hopeless sinners, only sheep that have wandered from the fold, and know not the way back; not useless and worthless human stuff, but souls that carried beneath the rust and grime the stamp of their birth, and might be put out at usury; not outcasts whose death would be a good riddance, but children loved and missed in their Father's House. This wreck, Jesus perpetually insisted, is not the man—only his lower self, ignorant, perverted, corrupt; the other self lies hidden and must be released. That is the real self, and when it is released you come to the man. 'When he came to himself,' said Jesus of the prodigal. This was Jesus' reading of publicans and sinners,—the pariahs of that civilisation. He moved among the people with a sanguine expectation; ever demanding achievements of the most unlikely, never knowing when He might not be gladdened by a response. An unwavering and unbounded faith in humanity sustained His heart and transformed its subjects.

Zacchæus, the hated tax-gatherer, makes a vast surrender, and shows also that he is a son of Abraham. St. Mary Magdalene, the byword of society, has in her the passion of a saint. St. Matthew abandons a custom-house to write a Gospel. St. John leaves his nets to become the mystic of the ages. St. Peter flings off his weakness, and changes into the rock of the Church. With everything against him, Jesus treated men as sons of God, and His optimism has had its vindication.

Jesus' attitude of hope rested also on His ideal of Life. His own disciples could not enter into His mind or see with His eyes. Modern reformers have sadly missed His standpoint. Laden with reproach and injury, He seemed to His friends the victim of intolerable ill-usage. As the Cross loomed in sight they besought Him to save Himself. They pitied Him who did not pity Himself; they were furious for Him who was Himself satisfied. For life with Jesus was not meat and drink, nor ease and honour. It was the perfection of the soul, and the way unto this high goal was the Cross. If suffering was the will of God, then it is a good in disguise; if it be the discipline of holiness, it is to be welcomed. The Son of Man must be crucified before He can rise in power. He must fall as a corn of wheat into the ground before He can bring forth much fruit. This was the order of things for Him and for all men, and out of the baptism of fire men will come clean souls. Jesus did not ignore the black shadow of sin; He did not fall into the sickly optimism of last century. Jesus did not regard man as the sport of a cruel Fate; He did not yield to the gloomy pessimism which is settling down on this dying century. He illuminated the darkness of human misery with the light of a Divine purpose, and made the evidence for despair an argument for hope.

It must be admitted that Jesus had moods, and in one of them He sometimes lost heart. One cannot forget the gloom of certain parables:—the doom of the fruitless tree; the execution of the wicked husbandman; the casting out of the unprofitable servant; the judgment on the uncharitable. He once doubted whether there would be faith at His coming; He prophesied woe to Capernaum; He wept over Jerusalem; He poured out His wrath on the Pharisees. But it was not about the world—the Samaritan woman, the mother from Tyre, the Roman centurion—His faith failed. It was about the Church—the Priests, the Scribes, the Pharisees, the Rulers. It remains for ever a solemn warning that while the Church is continually tempted to lose hope of the world, the one section of humanity of which Jesus despaired was the Church.

When one turns for facts to verify Jesus' optimism, the handiest, although not the most conclusive, is the growth of the Christian Church. The Church is to the kingdom what the electric current is to electricity. It is the kingdom organised for worship and aggression; it is the kingdom coming to a point and reduced to machinery. You could have the kingdom without the Church, and that day may come; you could have no Church without the kingdom. The Church is a rough index of the spread and vitality of the kingdom, and no one can deny that the history of the Church has been the outstanding phenomenon of modern times. It began with a handful of Jewish peasants, cast out by their own nation, and it embarked on a march of unparalleled conquest. From Jerusalem to Antioch, from

Q

Antioch to Asia, from Asia to Rome, this new unworldly faith made its victorious way, and from Rome to the ends of the earth. There is almost no land now where the Church has not sent her missionaries, has not planted her standard, has not enrolled her converts ; and if there be such, it is watched with greedy eyes. Her weakness, her failings, her blunders, her sins, have been patent to all, but they have only served to prove how prolific were the sources that recruited her shattered ranks, how constant the force that made itself felt through so imperfect an instrument. There are great religions on the earth besides the Church, but they have seen their best days, and have begun to decay. The faith of Jesus is moving to its zenith. There are strong empires to-day dividing the world between them, but none will venture to say that one of them is so likely to live as the Church Catholic. Her increase may be by thousands or millions, but it is evident she has no serious rival to dispute her final triumph, no hopeless hindrance save her own coldness.

But no one can have understood Jesus, who concludes that the Church embraces the king-

dom of God. Are there not many persons who
have no formal connection with the Church,
and yet are keeping the commandments of
Jesus, and have the likeness of His character?
They have not been baptized in His Name,
but they follow in His steps; they do not
show forth His Name, but they die daily in His
service. They have been born into a Christian
atmosphere; they have inherited the Christian
nature; they have responded to the Christian
spirit. What is one to say about these Samaritans? They do not answer to their names at
the temple with the Priests and Levites, and
therein they may have suffered loss; but they
show well on the roadside where the sick man
is lying. What did Jesus mean by His marked
approbation of the Samaritans? It was not
that He thought them right in their separation
from the Jewish Church, and He spoke plainly
on that matter to the Samaritan woman. It
was to show that life was deeper than forms,
and that incorrect doctrine may be consistent
with the noblest character.

The kingdom Jesus imagined is wider even
than the sphere of Christendom, and extends
where men have owed nothing to the subtle

strain of Christian heredity. In that great
Mogul Emperor Akbar, who in the sixteenth
century had discovered the principle of religious toleration : those Moslem saints whose fine
charity is embodied in the legend of Abou-ben-
Adhem : in the renunciation of Buddha, the
light of Asia : that Roman Emperor, whom
the young men called 'Marcus my father,' the
old men 'Marcus my son,' the men of middle
age 'Marcus my brother,'—in such lives one
recognises the distinctive qualities of the kingdom. It is surely a narrow mind, and worse—
a narrow heart—that would belittle the noble
sayings that fell from the lips of outside saints
or discredit the virtues of their character. Is
it not more respectful to God, the Father of
mankind, and more in keeping with the teaching of the Son of Man, to believe that everywhere and in all ages can be found not only
the prophecies and broken gleams, but also the
very children of the kingdom? In Clement's
noble words, 'Some with the consciousness
of what Jesus is to them, others not as yet ;
some as friends, others as faithful servants,
others barely as servants.'

The Sermon on the Mount is the measure of

Jesus' optimism, and its gradual fulfilment His justification. His ideas have matured in the human consciousness, and are now bursting into flower before our eyes. Thoughtful men of many schools are giving their mind to the programme of Jesus, and asking whether it ought not to be attempted. The ideal of Life, one dares now to hope, is to be realised within measurable distance, and the dreams of the Galilean Prophet become history.

When the kingdom comes in its greatness, it will fulfil every religion and destroy none, clearing away the imperfect and opening up reaches of goodness not yet imagined, till it has gathered into its bosom whatsoever things are true and honest and just and pure and lovely. It standeth on the earth as the city of God with its gates open by night and by day, into which entereth nothing that defileth, but into which is brought the glory and power of the nations. It is the natural home of the good; as Zwingli, the Swiss reformer, said in his dying confession, 'Not one good man, one holy spirit, one faithful soul, whom you will not then behold with God.'

FATHERHOOD THE FINAL
IDEA OF GOD

ence proves its effect. As the light of the sun colours the tiniest blade of grass, so the idea in the background of the mind tinges every detail of life. We grant that a man's theology will be built on his belief, and will follow its lines to the highest pinnacle. This is a grudging concession, a limited analysis. The whole energy of a human life, however it may have been fed on the way, and whatever common wheels it may turn, arises from the spring among the hills. Belief gives the trend to politics, constitutes the rule of business, composes the atmosphere of home, and creates the horizon of the soul. It becomes the sovereign arbiter of our destinies, for character itself is the precipitate of belief.

Belief, within the sphere of religion, has a wide range, but its centre is God. Tell me what is your conception of God, and I will work out your doctrine of man, of forgiveness, of life, of punishment. Given the axioms, and geometry is only a question of process. Given your God, and your whole theology can be constructed within a measurable time. The chief service of a prophet is not to rebuke sin, nor instruct in virtue : it is to give the world a radiant idea of God. Has he no word on God? Then his silence is irreparable—every other doctrine will be isolated and fruitless. Has he a fitting idea of God? Then his blank chapters can be supplied; they are contained in the introduction. If a prophet deal after a satisfying fashion with the idea of God, he will be permanent. If a prophet complete and crown the idea of God, he will be final. Many may expound him: none can transcend him. Jesus taught the world various principles of religion —the nature of faith, the glory of sacrifice, the secret of peace, the strength of love. These were the splendid incidents of His Gospel. The Gospel of Jesus was the revelation of God.

Jesus availed Himself of what existed, and began with the assumption of God. He never fell into the banality of theology, and set Himself to prove the existence of God, which is as if a geologist should introduce his science with an argument for the reality of the world. When one has to begin before the beginning, he is filled with despair, for that way lies madness. We are entitled to take some things for granted, as, for instance, the evidence of our senses and the teaching of an instinct. Belief in God is an instinct, a part of the constitution of the soul. It may be confirmed and illustrated: it must not be proved, for the proof of an instinct is its denial. When Jesus said God He appealed to the belief latent in every human being, and called it into a nobler exercise. He did not create the idea of God—He illumined it.

Jesus availed Himself also of what had been done, and accepted that character of God, which was the discovery of ancient piety. As the belief in God began with the first father of the Race, the doctrine of God began with the Hebrew saints. Long centuries before Jesus, patriarchs and prophets had been wrestling with the problems of the Divine Being and the Divine Name. With the sword of faith and great travail of soul, those pioneers of religion had conquered, foot by foot, the land of promise, and left it as an heritage unto their children. They had extricated the idea of God from the work of men's hands and the phenomena of nature: in later days the pious Jew guarded it from the abstractions of philosophy and the corrosion of scepticism. This monotheism was not the natural tendency of the

Semite, born of the desert environment—that ingenious naturalistic theory is now exploded; it was the slow, painful attainment of Hebrew faith reinforced by the Divine Spirit. We owe the 'Living God' to the Jew, and as often as this sublime conception is obscured or sapped by the eccentricities of modern speculation, the religious consciousness must fall back on the masculine vigour and ethical grandeur of Old Testament thought.

The genius of the Jewish mind was not metaphysical; it could not have produced the Athanasian Creed: it was ethical; it is embodied in the Ten Words. With the Jew, therefore, God was not abstract Being—the First Cause of things. He was actual character, the 'Holy One of Israel.' Jehovah dwelt in the high and holy place, and with him also of a humble and contrite heart; and if He 'maketh the clouds His chariot,' and 'walketh upon the wings of the winds,' His 'righteousness is like the great mountains,' His 'judgments are a great deep.' There grew in the consciousness of this people the idea of a God who was not only real—no carved and painted log of prophetical satire, but also moral—no complacent deity tasting the

sweetness of his worshippers' sins. They verified His character in the disasters that followed
national corruption, in the swift recoveries that
rewarded national repentance. In the mirror
of a cleansed conscience the prophets saw the
face of God; they traced His life in the processes of righteousness. We fail sometimes to
appreciate the force of this discovery; we forget
to imagine the surprise. With moderns, Deity
and virtue are synonymous; with ancients,
deities and vice were synonymous. Upon two
hills only was the Divine raised above the

'Howling senses' ebb and flow.'

One was the Acropolis where the golden shaft
in Athene's hand guided the mariner passing
Salamis. The other was the Holy Hill where
Jehovah remained the refuge of every righteous
man. But the advantage lay with the Jew.
The wisdom of Athens was seated in reason,
and did not affect life: the wisdom of Jerusalem was seated in conscience, and created conduct. The Jewish Savonarola who thundered
in Jerusalem, 'Wash you, make you clean; put
away the evil of your doings from before mine
eyes,' had come out from a secret place where

the Seraphim said, 'Holy, holy, holy is the Lord of Hosts.'

Jewish piety has laid the world under a hopeless debt by imagining the austere holiness of God, and has doubled the obligation by adding His tenderness. It was an achievement to carve the white marble; a greater to make it live and glow. The saints of Israel touched their highest when they infused the idea of the Divine spirituality with passion, and brought it to pass that the Holy One of Israel is the kindest deity that has ever entered the heart of man. There was no human emotion they did not assign to God; no relationship they did not use as the illustration of His love; no appeal of affection they did not place in His lips; no sorrow of which they did not make Him partaker. When a prophet's inner vision had been cleansed by the last agony of pain, he dares to describe the Eternal as a fond mother who holds Ephraim by the hands, teaching him to go; who is outraged by his sin, and yet cannot bear that Israel should perish: as a Husband who has offered a rejected love, and still pleads; who is stained by a wife's unfaithfulness, and pursues an adulteress with entreaties. One cannot lay his hand on the body of prophetical Scripture without feeling the beat of the Divine heart: one can detect in its most distant member the warmth of the Divine love.

Your first conclusion is that faith can go no farther: your second reading reveals one significant reserve. Prophets continually call God the Father of the nation; they never (with one doubtful exception) call Him Father of the individual. Psalmists revel in an overflowing imagery for God, but one word lying to their hand they do not use. He is the 'Shepherd of Israel' and 'our dwelling-place in all generations'; He is the 'Rock of my Salvation' and a 'very present help in trouble': He is the 'Health of my countenance,' and 'thy shade on thy right hand'; but He is not Father. King is the Psalmists' chief title for God and his highest note. 'The Lord reigneth.' These saints are unapproachable in their familiarity with the Eternal; they will argue and complain; they will demand and reproach, but never at any moment are they so carried beyond themselves as to say 'My Father.' They are bold within a limit: they have restraints in their language. It is not a refusal to say Father, because the

idea is an offence : it is an unconsciousness—
because the idea has not yet dawned. The
clouds which had gradually risen from the base
and sides of the doctrine of God still veil the
summit.

When one passes from the Gospels to the
Psalms he is struck by the absence of Father.
When one returns he is struck by its presence.
The Psalmist never said the word ; Jesus never
said anything else. With Jesus, God and
Father were identical. Fatherhood was not a
side of Deity; it was the centre. God might
be a King and Judge; He was first of all, and
last of all, and through all, Father. In Fatherhood every other relation of God must be
harmonised and find its sphere. Short of His
Fatherhood you cannot stop in the ascent of
God. Under Fatherhood is gathered every
other revelation. Jesus reasoned in terms of
the Father: 'If ye then, being evil, know how
to give good gifts unto your children, how
much more shall your Father which is in
heaven give good things to those that ask
Him ?' He laboured in the fellowship of the
Father: 'I seek not Mine own will, but the
will of the Father which hath sent Me.' He

R

rested in the wisdom of the Father: 'In that hour Jesus rejoiced in spirit, and said, I thank Thee, O Father, Lord of heaven and earth, that Thou hast hid these things from the wise and prudent, and hast revealed them unto babes: even so, Father; for so it seemed good in Thy sight.' And Jesus suffered in the faith of the Father: 'Therefore doth My Father love Me because I lay down My life that I might take it again. . . . This commandment have I received of My Father.' When the consciousness of God awoke with power in the soul of the Holy Child, He was filled with a sudden enthusiasm, 'Wist ye not that I must be about My Father's business?' When He had fulfilled His calling and offered His sacrifice, His soul turned to His Father: 'Father, into Thy hands I commend My Spirit.' From Nazareth to Calvary the love of the Father was Jesus' dwelling-place.

> 'In that one thought He abode
> For ever in that thought more deeply sinking.'

No one can ignore this constant and radiant sense of the Divine Fatherhood in the life of Jesus. It must be a suggestive fact to an un-

believer, for it will be admitted on every hand
that Jesus knew more about Religion than any
man that has ever lived. It ought to be an absolute conclusion to a believer, since he holds
that Jesus is Himself Very God of Very God.

It goes without saying that Jesus' sense of
the Fatherhood must be supreme. It is a contradiction of the Gospels to say that it was exclusive. Jesus toiled for three years to write
the truth of the Fatherhood on the minds of
the disciples, with at least one result, that it is
interwoven with the pattern of the Gospels.
He pleaded also with His friends that they
should receive it into their hearts till St. John
filled his epistles with this word. With minute
and affectionate care, Jesus described the whole
circle of religious thought, and stated it in
terms of the Fatherhood. Prayer was to be to
the Father: say 'Our Father, which art in
heaven.' The principle of life was the Will of
the Father: he only attained who had done
the 'Will of our Father which is in heaven.'
The type of character was the Father: 'Be ye
therefore perfect, even as your Father which is
in heaven is perfect.' Providence is the mind-
ful oversight of a Father: 'Your heavenly

Father knoweth that ye have need of all these things.' Repentance was a return to the Father: 'I will arise and go to my father.' One of the few rays Jesus cast on the future showed the Father's dwelling-place: 'In My Father's house are many mansions.' The effect of such passages is cumulative and irresistible. They are better than the proof texts for a dogma; they are an atmosphere in which religion lives and moves and has its being. They are sunrise.

People with dogmatic ends to serve have striven to believe that Jesus reserved Father for the use of His disciples; but an ingenuous person could hardly make the discovery in the Gospels. One searches in vain to find that Jesus had an esoteric word for His intimates, and an exoteric for the people, saying Father to John and Judge to the publicans. It had been amazing if Jesus were able to employ alternatively two views of God according to His audience, speaking now as an Old Testament Prophet, now as the Son of God. It is recorded in the Gospels, 'Then spake Jesus to the multitude and His disciples, saying, . . . one is your Father, which is in heaven.' This attempt to restrict the intention of Jesus is not of yesterday; it was the invention of the Pharisees. They detected the universal note in Jesus' teaching; they resented His unguarded charity. Their spiritual instincts were not wide, but they were very keen, within a limited range, and the Pharisees judged with much correctness that the teaching of Jesus and the privileges of Judaism were inconsistent. If a publican was a son of God, what advantage had a Pharisee? It was natural that they should murmur: we are now thankful that they criticised the Master. Jesus made His defence in His three greatest parables, and in the Parable of the Prodigal Son He defined the range of the Divine Fatherhood beyond reasonable dispute. His deliverance was given with deliberation—in Jesus' most finished parable; the parable was created for a definite purpose—to vindicate Jesus' intercourse with sinners. It contains Jesus' most complete description of a sinner—from his departure to his return; with emphasis it declares that sinner a son of God—a 'son was lost and is found.' Between the son in the far country and the son at home is an immense difference; but if

he had not been a son from home, there had
been no home for his return. The possibility
of salvation lies in sonship. It would not be
fair to rest any master doctrine on a single parable, were it not that the parable is Jesus'
definition of Fatherhood, given in answer to
the practical challenge of privilege, were it not
that it simply crystallises the whole teaching
of Jesus on God from His boyhood to His
death. If Jesus did not teach a Divine
Fatherhood embracing the Race, then He used
words to conceal thought, and one despairs of
ever understanding our Master.

When Jesus speaks of Fatherhood, it is almost a stupidity to explain that He is not
thinking of any physical relation—the 'offspring' of the heathen poets, and that Father
is not a synonym for Creator. Jesus rested
His own Sonship on community of character.
God was love, for He gave His only Son, and
Jesus was love, for He gave Himself. He realised His Sonship in community of service.
'My Father worketh hitherto, and I work.'
The bond between son and father in the spiritual world is ethical. It is perfect between the
Father and the Son in the Holy Trinity: it is

only a suggestion between a sinner and God. As one can detect some trace of likeness between a father and his son, although the son may have played the fool, and defiled the fashion of his countenance, so the most degraded and degenerate of human outcasts still bears the faint remains of the Divine image. The capability of repentance is the remains of righteousness; the occasional aspirations after goodness are the memories of home; the recognition of right and wrong is an affinity to the mind of God. The sonship is hidden in Zaccheus and Mary Magdalene—a mere possibility; in St. John and St. Paul it is revealed—a beautiful actuality, so that this paradox is only the deeper truth that one may be, and yet become, a son, as the ethical likeness is acknowledged and cleansed. Jesus' message was, 'You are a son.' As soon as it was believed, Jesus gave power to live as a son with God.

With this single word 'Father,' Jesus instantly defines the relation of man and God, and illuminates theology. He transfers the Divine idea from the schools, where they discuss the Sovereignty of God, to the hearth, where the little children can say 'Our Father' with understanding. It was a felicitious image which suddenly appropriated for theology the analogies of love and the associations of home; which teaches us to argue with irresistible force what my father on earth would not do because it is evil my Father in heaven will not do; what my father here will do of good, that and more my Father above will do. Granted that this is anthropomorphic reasoning, how else can we argue than from the good in us to the better in God? Granted that this analogy is faint, that only invests it with more winsome attraction. What an astounding *gaucherie* it has been to state the intimate relation between God and the soul in the language of criminal law, with bars, prisoners, sentences. This terminology has two enormous disadvantages. It is unintelligible to any one who is not a criminal or a lawyer; it is repulsive to any one who desires to love God. Take it at the highest, it was the spirit of Moses. Without disparagement to a former dispensation, it has been superseded by the spirit of Jesus.

One is not astonished that some of Jesus' deepest sayings are still unfathomed, or that some of His widest principles are not yet applied. Jesus is the Eternal Son, and the ages overtake Him slowly. One is aghast to discover that the doctrine which Jesus put in the forefront of His teaching and laboured at with such earnestness did not leave a trace on the dominant theology of the early Church, and for long centuries passed out of the Christian consciousness. Had it not been for the Lord's Prayer and, in a sense, the three Creeds, no witness had been left for the Fatherhood in Christian doctrine and worship. The Anglican communion has thirty-nine articles, with one on oaths, one on the descent into hell, one on the marriage of priests, one on how to avoid people that are excommunicate, and not one on the Fatherhood. The Presbyterian communion has a confession with thirty-three chapters, which deal in a trenchant manner with great mysteries, but there is not one expounding the Fatherhood of God. It was quite allowable that theology should formulate doctrines on subjects Jesus never mentioned, such as original sin ; and elaborate theories on facts Jesus left in their simplicity, such as His sacrifice. These speculations are the function of that science, but it is inexcusable that the central theme of

Jesus' teaching should have been ignored or minimised. This silence, from the date of the Greek fathers to the arrival of the modern Broad Churchman, has been more than an omission; it has been a heresy.

It is an endless consolation that our Master's words are indestructible and eternal. Certain ideas of Jesus disappeared, and seemed to have died; they were not dead, they were only sown. When their due time came they awoke to life, and it is now spring-time with the Fatherhood. The disciples of Jesus owe a debt that can never be paid to three men that have brought us back to the mind of our Master. One was Channing, for whose love to Jesus one might be tempted to barter his belief; the second was Maurice, most honest and conscientious of theologians; and the third was Erskine of Linlathen, who preached the Fatherhood to every one he met, from Thomas Carlyle to Highland shepherds. This sublime truth received at first the same treatment from the nineteenth century as from the first. Its inherent grace has not been an immediate commendation; its utter reasonableness has been an indirect provocation. But the spirit of Jesus has been working in men age after age, and it is now evident that the name for God that lay in Jesus' heart is to be acclimatised in the Christian consciousness.

Two persons hesitate to accept the Fatherhood in its fulness who are neither biassed by spiritual pride nor are disloyal to Jesus. With one it is an ethical difficulty, that stands in the way; he has a rooted suspicion that the assertion of God's Fatherhood means the denial of His authority, and that we shall exchange the Holy One of Israel for a magnified Eli. Certain advocates of Jesus' idea have themselves to blame for this misapprehension, since they have invested the 'Holy Father' of Jesus, whose Name is 'hallowed,' with a cloud of sickly sentiment, making Him a God too weak to rule, too soft-hearted to punish. If this conception should obtain, Christianity would deserve to lose her hold on the conscience, and morality would have to fight for very existence. Jesus is not responsible for this helpless Deity, this pitiable descent from the God of the prophets. With Jesus, the Father was Lord of heaven and earth, who 'seeth in secret,' and holds the times in His hand, who has not only prepared the 'many mansions,' but also the cleansing fires of Gehenna. No judge is so omniscient as a father, no despot so absolute. The Father of the Sermon on the Mount is not less awful than the God of the Ten words, nor is the conscience of St. John less strenuous than the conscience of Moses.

The second objection is practical, and carries much force, for it simply comes to this, that experience is a denial of the Fatherhood. One admires the Galilean dreamer with his Father-God, and His charming illustrations of the lilies and the birds, but this one says is an idyll, and life is real. What signs of paternal government can be found in the martyrdom of man from the first days of history to the last war, in the hideous sufferings of slavery, or in the equal miseries of great cities? With such a record before one, it is certainly open to argue that Jesus was too optimistic. Granted, but that does not close the question. With the record of His own life before one, it is not open to conclude Jesus was wrong. He drank the bitterest cup; He suffered the shamefullest death, and yet reconciled the incalculable tragedy of His life with the love of His Father.

Jesus did not regard suffering as the contradiction of love; it was one of its methods. When Jesus said Father on the Cross, it may have been a pathetic delusion, but it was the delusion of Him who of all the Race knew God best.

One joyfully anticipates the place this final idea of God will have in the new theology. Criticism has cleared the ground and gathered its building materials. A certain conception of God must be the foundation and give shape to the whole structure. No one can seriously doubt that it will be the Fatherhood, and that Jesus' dearest thought will dominate theology. No doctrine of the former theology will be lost; all will be recarved and refaced to suit the new architecture. Sovereignty will remain, not that of a despot, but of a father; the Incarnation will not be an expedient, but a consummation; the Sacrifice will not be a satisfaction, but a reconciliation: the end of Grace will not be standing, but character; the object of punishment will not be retribution, but regeneration. Mercy and justice will no longer be antinomies; they will be aspects of Love, and the principle of human probation will be exchanged for the principle of human education.

One sees already the place which the Father-hood will have in the new life into which the race in every land is entering. While piety imagined God as the Father of a few and the Judge of the rest, humanity was belittled and Pharisaism reigned; slavery was defended from the Bible, and missions were counted an imper-tinence. When He is recognised as the uni-versal Father, and the outcasts of Humanity as His prodigal children, every effort of love will be stimulated, and the Kingdom of God will advance by leaps and bounds. As this sublime truth is believed, national animosities, social divisions, religious hatreds and inhuman doctrines will disappear. No class will regard itself as favoured: no class will feel itself re-jected, for all men everywhere will be embraced in the mission of Jesus and the love of the Father.

THE FORESIGHT OF FAITH

THE FORESIGHT OF FAITH

The difference between the eternal vision of God and the temporal outlook of man has been compared to one standing on a hill with the landscape in its length and breadth before him, and another crossing the plain in a swiftly moving train, on whom the landscape breaks part by part. This ingenious illustration, after it has served its purpose to show the relation of eternity and time, may be utilised to suggest that we also have an eternal kinship. We retain what we have seen after it has vanished; we anticipate what has yet to be seen before it appears. It is the present which is not yet ours, since it is only being transferred to the exposed plate of experience—the past and the future are carried in our consciousness. One faculty of our mysterious nature records, as by an automatic register, the experiences of yesterday, so

S

that not one deed, or word, or thought is lost—
not one but can be reproduced by some commonplace spell, the crowing of a cock at early
dawn, or the fragrance of dried rose-leaves in
some old-fashioned drawing-room. Another
pictures with minute prophetic power the experiences of to-morrow, so that the distant horizon is golden with inspiring illusions, or black
with brooding anxieties. We are the slaves of
memory and imagination, but in the conflict for
the control of the soul imagination is easily vic-
tor. Hope rather than repentance is the instrument of salvation.

Imagination is the faculty which represents
the future, foresight is the quality which possesses it; and foresight is one of the standards
of character. Without foresight no one can
claim to be of serious account—he may take
lessons from an ant; with it no one need despair of any achievement—he has outrun time.
Foresight confers distinction on every effort of
man, and raises it a degree. It elevates economy into providence; it broadens business into
enterprise; with this addition politics become
statesmanship, and literature prophecy. Life
gains perspective and atmosphere; it is rein-

forced by unseen hopes and rewards. The burden of the future becomes a balance in life, tem-
pering the intoxication of joy with the cares of
to-morrow, and softening the bitterness of sorrow with its compensations. Foresight, sending on its spies into the land of promise, returns
to brace and cheer every power of the soul, and
becomes the mother of all hardy and strenuous
virtues, a self-restraint, and self-denial, of sacrifice and patience. He who seizes to-day may
have pleasure; he who grasps to-morrow shall
have power.

An admirable work of modern art shows
Jesus standing at the door of a carpenter's shop,
and stretching Himself after a long day's labour.
The setting sun falling on His outspread arms
makes the shadow of the cross, and carries ter-
ror into Mary's heart. The attitude of the
body was typical of the attitude of the soul.
Jesus grasped at the future, as He seemed also
to carry with Him a mysterious past. Before
Him extended the long distances of the Divine
Will, and He arranged His life for Calvary.
When a pious scholar came by night to discuss
His new ideas, Jesus could not explain the
Kingdom of God without a reference to His

cross. As He spake in the synagogue of Capernaum after the miracle of the loaves, His sacrifice rose before Him, and the bread of life became His Flesh and His Blood. On the way to Jerusalem He drew His disciples aside, and, while the people passed in their carelessness, Jesus described the tragedy that was at hand. The sight of certain foreign Jews, full of curiosity about this new Master, suggested to Him that throne from which He was to rule the world, and He saw across His Passion the victory of His Love. In the upper room His vision had passed beyond the cross, and He commanded that the sacrament of His Body and Blood should be celebrated till His second advent. After His resurrection He gave the first earnest of the Holy Ghost, and anticipated the spread of the Evangel throughout the world. With Jesus the present was ever eclipsed by the future, so that while the multitude would have made Him a King, He saw Himself forsaken on a cross ; and while He was about to be crucified, He was promising to return for the judgment of the world. He set His face stedfastly, lifted above the ebb and flow of circumstances, because the Divine Will was ever revealing itself, peak above peak, to the ages of ages.

Possessed by the spirit of to-morrow, it was natural that our Master should labour to imbue His disciples with the same; but on a first reading His teaching presents a perplexing paradox. This Man, who was born amid the narrow circumstances of poverty, and acquainted with its exacting cares, belittles ordinary prudence to an audience of country folk, and gives counsels of perfection about an easy mind. With the scanty wages of Galilee, and the charge of little children, they were to allow to-morrow to take care of itself, and not even concern themselves about the bare necessaries of life. He saw His chosen disciples fling away their only means of livelihood with approval, and sent them forth on a mission, as bare as the monks of St. Francis. If a young man won His love, He did not hesitate to demand the sacrifice of his possessions, and He pursued, with bitter mocking, rich men who doubled their investments. As for Himself, He was dependent on the charity of pious women, and had to work a miracle to pay the temple tax. He seems to justify the light heart of imprudence, and the recklessness of impulse, to condemn prudence as unbelief, and enterprise as crass foolishness.

Parallel with this depreciation of foresight, runs an endless exhortation to its practice. The Kingdom of God as the Chief Good is to be the first object in life; it is the pearl of great price which one ought to secure as the best of all his possessions. It was wisdom to humble one's self as a little child, because the child-character stood highest in the coming State; and better to take the lowest room at the feast of life, since the lowest would be the highest in the end. If one did sell all he had for Christ's sake, he would have treasure in heaven; and they who abandoned their best in His service, had the promise of a hundred-fold return. It was shrewder to labour for the Living Bread than for the meat that perisheth, because it would endure; and to place one's capital in heaven rather than on earth, because of the moth and rust which corrupt, and the thieves which break through and steal. Lazarus, with his good things on the other side, has the advantage over Dives with his brief while of purple and fine linen; and as a mere matter of profit and loss, he that saves his soul is wiser than he who gains a world. Jesus amazes us twice, first by casting the principle of prudence out of common life and making no provision for the future; and second, by introducing the principle of prudence into the sphere of religion, and making the rewards of the Kingdom of heaven a subject of calculation.

Let us remember that one of Jesus' most convincing characteristics was a certain soundness of mind, which kept Him continually in contact with fact and life. He accepted creation before proceeding to regeneration, and preferred to utilise human nature rather than quarrel with it. Foresight is an instinct which is atrophied in criminals and wastrels, which flourishes in workers and rulers. It may be cultivated either within the sphere of the seen or the unseen, and as a matter of fact has seldom been adopted by faith. With two worlds before His eye, Jesus proposed to shift the *venue* of this influential motive from this world into that which is to come, and sought to accomplish the change by starving foresight, when expended upon the material, and fostering it when devoted to the spiritual. As it is evidently out of the question that one can

make the best of both worlds—ye cannot serve
God and Mammon, as our Master said in His
conclusive way—Jesus desired that His disciples should concentrate themselves upon the
world which remaineth.

Jesus embodied His comparative view of
material and spiritual foresight in a parable
which has a double distinction. The Unjust
Steward is the only parable of Jesus which
gives for one instant a shock of moral offence
to the reader; it is also the only one which
illustrates the action of the principle of foresight on two different ethical levels. It is quite
allowable for us to be surprised that Jesus
should choose a case of deliberate and clever
fraud for a parable; it is scarcely pardonable
that any intelligent person should suppose that
Jesus approved or condoned the fraud. One is
indeed struck by Jesus' felicity in selecting a
set of circumstances which will so certainly
excite intellectual curiosity, and so perfectly
bring out His point. Within the briefest
space the place of foresight in human action
is defined, while its lower application is
skilfully depreciated, and its higher power
fully enforced. It is Jesus' most incisive de-

liverance on worldliness, and other-worldliness.

The parable is a palimpsest whose surface presents a story in commercial life, so ignoble and uninviting that it does not deserve record, and contains beneath half-hidden, half-revealed, a gospel of Jesus. But this palimpsest has a peculiarity of its own, because the upper legend is not an obliteration of the lower truth, but rather its introduction—the envelope which holds the message. One ought not to erase the legend before he has mastered it, because in that case he will miss the key to the interpretation of the truth. This indolent and luxurious steward, without conscience or manliness, is the lowest type of a man of this world. The unexpected discovery of his embezzlement, and his threatened dismissal from office, are the sudden changes which affect the ease and comfort of the present life. His vivid anticipations of the hardness of life for a poor and disgraced man show how selfishness can be served by imagination. And the fellow's fraudulent device is an example of insurance against coming risks, and of adaptation to new circumstances. Jesus did not choose an honourable merchant because He required the dismissal for His parable, and He desired to invest sheer worldliness with a dash of contempt. This was a petty rascal—a mere fox of a man—but he saved himself, according to his lights, by foresight.

The under writing on the parchment corresponds with the upper, save for one or two significant blanks, and is a translation of the same story into another language. This self-indulgent steward is replaced by the disciple of Jesus with his cross. Death will release him from this inhospitable life and restore him to his home. Yet his imagination has never realised what shall be the splendour of his spiritual environment. And he is not striving with all his might so to till the opportunities of this life that he shall reap their harvest in the life which is to come. That shallow trickster will sell his conscience to secure a roof above his head for a brief space; but Jesus' disciple will not bestir himself to make certain of everlasting habitations. It was to Jesus quite astonishing either that any one should take much thought what might befall him in this world which passeth away, or that any one should be indifferent to the infinite attraction of the world which abideth. The parable is a eulogium on foresight, and a plea that its whole force should be used to secure the 'everlasting habitations.' It is Jesus' argument for ' other-worldliness.'

It may be frankly admitted that a very coarse and sordid interpretation can be put on this argument, and the conduct of the unjust steward be repeated with aggravation on the spiritual side of things. The parable does lend itself to that material Theology whether of Rome or Geneva, which teaches that Heaven can be literally bought. Whether the price be the merits of Jesus or the merits of saints, the sufferings of Jesus or the alms of penitents, does not matter, since in either case the principle is the same and is clearly unreasonable. Heaven is a spiritual state and its settlement on any person, either on account of a payment in blood or money, is an absurdity. His introduction into this new environment without respect to his fitness would be an outrage. This is too literal a rendering of the steward's bookkeeping; too flagrant a contradiction of the whole spirit of Jesus' teaching. What is intended is different. Jesus' blood will give white robes which are the dress of Heaven: the faithful use of riches will produce character which is the passport to Heaven. One can imagine how the penitent thief might become suddenly fit for Paradise, because he did homage to goodness—when goodness was obscured by the shame and weakness of the cross. One cannot imagine Ananias obtaining entrance by the unwilling gift of all he possessed, or by an act of mercenary faith. Foresight will win Heaven, but it is not the foresight of a mercantile speculation.

One remembers at the same time that certain persons in the Gospels did use their earthly possessions after such a wise and gracious fashion that they proved themselves not unworthy to have a place in the Kingdom of Heaven, either in this world or the next. The Magi who brought their gifts to the Holy Child; the faithful women who made a home for God's Son; St. Matthew, and such as he, who left all to follow Him; Zaccheus, who in honour of His coming gave half of his goods to the poor; Joseph, who obtained Christ's body from Pilate and laid it in his own garden tomb, were good stewards. These men did make friends with

the mammon of unrighteousness, and changed
their gold and silver into eternal riches.   They
did not make their sacrifices for ends of gain,
but for love's sake.   Keeping the one commandment of Love, they had kept all the
others, and had a right to enter in by the gate
into the City.   This little handful saw farther
than all their generation, for in the things of
the Spirit foresight is not the cunning calculation of chances, it is rather the sacrifice of everything for Christ.   There are two passages which
go well together in the Gospels : one is ' Then
took Mary a pound of spikenard, very costly,
and anointed the feet of Jesus ' ; and the other,
' In my Father's house are many mansions . . .
I go to prepare a place for you.'

According to the mind of Jesus, the foresight
which prepares one for the future life is a certain attitude of soul.   No person, it may be assumed, would refuse the reversion of a blessed
future, with its high hopes of the freedom of
holiness and the unfettered service of the Divine Will, but many persons are not minded to
subordinate its unseen excellence to the solid
possession of the present.   They have made
themselves so absolutely at home among the

principles and rewards of a material world that they would be out of place amid the very different conditions and occupations of a spiritual world. It is this unfitness that will deny them a habitation. Certain persons, on the other hand, are determined that the physical shall not fling its 'tangling veil' so close around their hearts as to blind them to the glory of the Unseen, and are prepared to use the things which are seen as the stepping-stone to the things which are eternal. They store within their souls these intangible treasures of goodness, which are wrested from the experiences of sacrifice as pearls are from the dark caverns of the deep. With such gold they purchase their home in the Land of Promise. Their fitness will ensure their habitation.

> ' He who flagged not in the earthly strife,
> From strength to strength advancing only he,
> His soul well knit, and all his battles won,
> Mounts and that hardly to eternal life.'

Jesus approved the man who lived under the power of the Unseen, who was guided by a resolute, strenuous faith, who was determined not to lose the future. He had no hope of easy-going, thoughtless, improvident persons—the pauper class—in the spiritual world: from them he expected no great endeavours: for them he prophesied nothing but disasters. The man who had forethought built his house on the rock: the man who had none built his on the sand. The rock-house stood, the sand-house fell. The servant who played the fool because his master delayed his coming was cast out: had he persevered unto the end, he would have been accepted. It was the catastrophe of short-sightedness: he ought to have kept his master's coming before his eyes. Five virgins are re-solved that they will on no account miss the marriage, and make their arrangements at a cost of thought. Five have other things to think about besides the marriage, and do not burden themselves with preparations. Five enter in because for them the Kingdom of God was first: five remain outside because for them it was an ordinary matter. The wise virgins were of the same temper as Jesus Himself, and so they were His friends.

'Other-worldliness' has been the subject of much satire in our materialistic day, and has been condemned for its enervating and crippling influence on life. It is right, therefore, to re-

mind one's self that ' Other-worldliness' has two
forms and that both are not open to such
charges.   One school of piety has always held
that the choice preparation for the Eternal
World is seclusion and devotion, and when the
Second Advent was confidently expected, in
the middle ages, society was disorganised and
life arrested in Europe.   Western Christendom
was caught in a spasm of repentance, and even
irreligious people were shaken; some entered
sacred houses ; some hid themselves in caves ;
some set out for Palestine to meet the Lord.
The fruits of that brief emotion remain unto
this day in stately buildings and ecclesiastical
donations.   Yet about that very time some one
conceived a very lovely parable that also remaineth.   How a godly monk prayed and fasted
and longed to see Christ.   How one day a light
began to shine in his lonely cell, and he waited
for the visible revelation of his loved Lord ; how
at that very moment his summons came to feed
the poor at the convent gate ; how he obeyed
the call and gave out the loaves of bread and
returned in sorrow, for he was sure that he
had missed the condescension of the Lord ; and
how Christ was waiting for him, and said,

'Hadst thou refused thy duty, I had left ; since
thou wast faithful, I tarried to bless thee.
Two complimentary chapters in 'Other-worldliness.'

Charles V. of Spain was the greatest person-
age in the history of his day—the heir of four
royal lines, ruler of Spain, the Netherlands,
Austria and Naples, for whom Cortes had also
conquered the New World. He led huge ar-
mies, gained great victories, conducted momen-
tous affairs, lived amid critical events. In his
day the Ottoman was beaten back from the
frontiers of Europe and the Christian Church
was divided. It was in this wide place Charles
lived, amid these stirring circumstances he
moved; yet he was ever thinking of the end,
and had resolved, with Isabella, his loved
Queen, to retire at a certain time into a holy
place and wait for Christ. The Master came
for her before the day arrived, but Charles ab-
dicated his throne and divested himself of
power amid general sorrow and admiration, and
gave his last days to the practice of religion in
the Monastery of Yuste. Contrast with this
cloistered piety the scene in the American
Senate-house during the Revolution, when at

T

mid-day a great darkness fell and no man could see his brother's face. Even these stout Puritans were for the moment dismayed. Voices cried, 'It is the Day of Judgment,' and there was some confusion. Then one of the Fathers rose and said, 'Whether it be the Judgment Day or no, I know not, but this I know, that it is God's Will we save our country, and we shall be judged accordingly. I move that the candles be lit and that we go on with our business.' Two schools of 'Other-worldliness,' and very different. With the Catholic foresight spelt devotion—with the Puritan, duty.

It is an ungenerous task to compare these types of piety, and one ought to be grateful for each in its place. The Master is not likely to despise that delicate and reverent feeling which would wait for His coming in a secret place and meet Him in prayer. Nor is it to be thought that He will set any store by the mechanical performance of loveless service and exalt Judas with his bag above Mary with her spikenard. Jesus has wrought a beautiful harmony, for in one of His parables He has taken the most mystical form of 'Other-worldliness' —that which watches for His Second Advent,

and has laid on His waiting servant the most
homely task—to give to the household their
meat in due season. With one touch of grace
He has made duty a synonym for piety, and
has reconciled the inner and outer life. He
has vindicated the ' Other-worldliness' of the
Gospels, for He has made the foresight of the
Kingdom of God, in its loftiest ambition as
well as its minutest calculation, identical with
the unsparing and self-forgetful service of man.

THE CONTINUITY OF LIFE

THE CONTINUITY OF LIFE

When William Blake, the painter-poet, lay dying, he said ' he was going to that country he had all his life wished to see,' and just before he died ' he burst into singing of the things he saw.' It was the passion of a saint, whose heart had long been lifted above the present world ; it was the vision of a mystic, whose imagination had long been exercised on the world to come. Few outside the Bible succession have been inspired of the Holy Ghost like him who wrote the Songs of Innocence and illustrated the Epic of Job. But common men share in their measure this instinct of the eternal, this curiosity of the unseen. One must be afflicted with spiritual stupidity or cursed by incurable frivolity who has never thought of that new state on which he may any day enter, nor speculated concerning its conditions. Amid

the pauses of this life, when the doors are closed
and the traffic on the streets has ceased, our
thoughts travel by an irresistible attraction to
the other life. What like will it be, and what
will be its circumstances? What will be its
occupations and history? 'God forgive me,'
said Charles Kingsley, facing death, 'but I look
forward to it with an intense and reverent
curiosity.' He need not have asked pardon, for
he was fulfilling his nature.

One is not astonished that this legitimate
curiosity has created a literature, or that its
books can be divided into sheep and goats.
Whenever any province transcends experience
and is veiled in mystery, it is certain to be the
play of the childish and irresponsible fancy or
the subject of elaborate and semi-scientific
reasoning. Were it possible to place a foolscap
on one of our most sublime ideas, and turn immortality itself into an absurdity, it is done when
a vulgar imagination has peddled with the details of the future, and has accomplished a
travesty of the Revelation of St. John. From
time to time ignorant charlatans will trade on
religious simplicity and trifle with sacred emotions, whose foolishness and profanity go before

them unto judgment.   Heaven is the noblest imagination of the human heart, and any one who robs this imagination of its august dignity and spiritual splendour has committed a crime. Certain thoughtful and reverent writers, on the other hand, have addressed themselves to the future existence and its probable laws with a becoming seriousness and modesty.   The *Unseen Universe*, which was written by two eminent scientists, and Isaac Taylor's *Physical Theory of Another Life*, are books worthy of a great subject, and a fit offering on the altar of Faith.   Within a limited range science and philosophy are welcome prophets on the unseen, but at a point they leave us, and we stand alone, awestruck, fascinated, before the veil. No one has come from the other side and spoken with authority save Jesus.

One who believes in the pre-existence of our Master approaches the Gospels with high expectations and sustains a distinct disappointment.   Jesus' attitude to the other world is a sustained contradiction because His life reveals a radiant knowledge and His teaching preserves a rigid silence.   As Jesus moves through the Gospels, the sheen of Heaven is visible upon

Him. Above the mixed noises of earth the voice of the Eternal fell on His ear; beyond the hostile circle of Pharisees He saw the joy in the presence of God. Once and again came the word from heaven, 'This is my Beloved Son, in whom I am well pleased,' and in His straits the angels ministered unto Him. He lived so close to the frontier that His garments were once shot through with light, and His relations with the departed were so intimate that He spake with the past leaders of Israel concerning His mission. It does not surprise one that Jesus should suddenly disappear any more than that a bubble should rise to the surface of water, or that He ascended from the earth any more than that a bird should open its wings and fly. It was not strange that Jesus should pass into the unseen; it was strange that He should appear in the seen.

Jesus had established in His own Person that communication which ancient ages had desired, and modern science is labouring to attain. One may be pardoned for anticipating some amazing results—a more complete apocalypse. What unsuspected applications of natural law, what new revelations of spiritual knowledge, what immense reaches of Divine service, what boundless possibilities of life, might not Jesus have revealed in the sphere of the unseen. We search in vain for these open mysteries—this lifting of the veil from the occult. Whatever Jesus may have seen, and whatever He may have known, were locked in His breast,

> '. . . or something sealed
> The lips of that Evangelist.'

No believer in the pre-existence of Jesus can affect indifference to this silence; every one must desire some relief from its pressure. Most likely Jesus recognised that frequent references to the circumstances of the unseen world would have obscured one of the chief points in His teaching. He was ever insisting that the kingdom of heaven was no distant colony in the clouds, but an institution set up in this present world. He was ever hindered by the gross conceptions of the Jews, who could not compass any other Utopia than a conquering Messiah and a visible Theocracy. It was hard enough to cleanse the sight of His disciples from a religious imperialism, and to possess them with a vision of a spiritual society.

Had He once excited their imagination with an apocalypse of gold, then they had never grasped the fact that the kingdom of God is within, and they had been quite unsettled for the labour of its establishment. They must understand with all their hearts that where Jesus and the men of His Spirit were the Kingdom stood, whether in some obscure village of Galilee or in the many mansions of His Father's house. There are moods in which we should have liked a chapter on heaven from Jesus, in our wiser moments we see it would have been premature. When the Kingdom had been fairly founded on earth an apocalypse of glory would be a re-enforcement of hope. While the Kingdom was only an ideal it had been the destruction of faith.

Jesus broke His reserve on the last night of the three years' fellowship, when He was about to depart from His disciples' sight by the way of the Cross, and they would be left to face the world in His name. They had come together to the veil, and before He passed within, through His rent body, He must give His friends an assurance of the unseen that their hearts may not be troubled. As often as He

had spoken of the Ageless Life, He had touched on the life to come, now He gave His solitary deliverance on the sphere of that life, and
the form is characteristic of the Master.   There
could never be competition or comparison between Jesus and St. John; the magnificence of
the apocalypse fades before one simple word of
the last discourse.   Jesus utilises the great parable of the Family for the last time; and as
He had invested Fatherhood and Sonhood with
their highest meaning so He now spiritualises
Home.   What Mary's cottage at Bethany had
been to the little company during the Holy
Week, with its quiet rest after the daily turmoil
of Jerusalem; what some humble house on the
shore of Galilee was to St. John, with its associations of Salome; what the great Temple was
to the pious Jews, with its Presence of the
Eternal, that on the higher scale was Heaven.
Jesus availed Himself of a wealth of tender
recollections and placed Heaven in the heart
of humanity when He said, 'My Father's
House.'

It is, however, one thing to be silent about
the circumstances of the future and another to
be silent about its nature.   The reticence of

Jesus about the next world has an ample compensation in His suggestions regarding the next life.   Jesus was not indifferent to surroundings—He was grateful for the home at Bethany; Jesus was chiefly concerned about life— He counted it of the last importance to give a right direction to life.   During all His ministry Jesus was fighting ideas of life which were false, not so much because they were wicked as because they were temporary.   He was insisting on ideals of life which were true, not only because they were good but because they were eternal.   His conception of life was open to criticism just because it was so independent of time and space.   It was not national, it was human; it was not for His day, but for ever. You are impressed by the perspective in Jesus' teaching, the sense of beyond, and it is always spiritual.   Neither this world in its poverty nor the next in its wealth is to be compared with life, any more than a body with a soul.   The great loss of the present is to exchange your life for this world, the great gain in the world to come is still to obtain life.   The point of connection between the seen and the unseen— the only bridge that spans the gulf—is life.   In this state of things we settle its direction, in the next we shall see its perfection. According to the drift of Jesus' preaching, the whole spiritual content of this present life, its knowledge, skill, aspirations, character, will be carried over into the future, and life hereafter be the continuation of life here.

This assumption underlies Jesus' words at every turn, and comes to the surface in the parables of Service and Reward. They imply the continuity of life: they illuminate its conditions. The Master commits five talents to the servant, and the trust is shrewdly managed. The five become ten, and the Master is fully satisfied. What reward does He propose for His servant? Is it release from labour and responsibility—a future in contrast with the past? Is it, so to say, retirement and a pension? It would not be absurd, but it would be less than the best. Something more could surely be done with this man's exercised and developed gifts—his foresight, prudence, courage, enterprise. The past shapes the future, and this servant, having served his apprenticeship, becomes himself a master, 'ruler over many things.' So he entered into the joy of his Lord, and the joy for which Jesus endured the Cross is a patient and perpetual ministry. Life will be raised, not reversed; work will not be closed, it will be emancipated. The fret will be gone, not the labour; the disappointment, not the responsibility. Our disability shall be no more; our capacity shall be ours for ever, and so the thorns shall be taken from our crown.

This conception of the future as a continuation under new and unimaginable forms of present energy, has hardly been allowed full play. The religious mind has been dominated by a conventional idea which is taught to our children, which is assumed in conversation: which is implied in sermons, which inspires our hymnology on the 'Last Things.' Heaven is a state of physical rest—a release from care, labour, struggle, progress, which more thoughtful people represent to themselves as an endless contemplation of God, and less thoughtful reduce to an endless service of praise. We fulfil the Divine Will here in occupation, there we shall fulfil it in adoration. We shall leave the market-place with its arduous, yet kindly business, and enter a church where night and day

the ceaseless anthem swells up to the roof.
Upon this heaven the mystics, from St. John
to Faber, have lavished a wealth of poetry,
which we all admire and sing, and this is its
sum :—

> ' Father of Jesus, love's reward,
>   What rapture will it be
> Prostrate before Thy throne to lie
>   And gaze and gaze on Thee.'

It is the Christian Nirvana.

If this Paradise of inaction be the true idea
of Heaven, then it invites serious criticism.
For one thing, it can have only a lukewarm attraction for average people (who are the enormous majority of the race), and may be repug-
nant to those who are neither unbelieving nor
evil-living. Cloistered piety may long for this
kind of life as the apotheosis of the monastic
ideal, but all God's children are not cast in the
mould of À Kempis. What, for instance, can
an English merchant, a respectable, clean-liv-
ing, and fairly intelligent man, we shall suppose, think of the conventional Heaven? He
will not tell any one, because a sensible man
rarely gives confidences on religion, and he
may feel it wise to crush down various

thoughts. But one has a strong sense of incongruity between the life he lives here and the life it is supposed he will live hereafter, and this without reflection on his present useful and honourable way of living. One imagines how he will miss his office, and his transactions, and his plans, and his strokes of success, not because he has lost the machinery for making money, but because he misses the sphere for his strongest powers—his shrewdness, perseverance, enterprise, integrity. It were ludicrous to suggest that this excellent man, even in his old age, longs for death as the passage to that new world where he may begin life afresh, or that he wishes to be set free from the duties of this world that he may give himself, without hindrance, to the exercises of devotion. If he were to tell you so, you would detect the unreality, but in justice to this type, he does not cant when death comes to his door. He will brace himself, as a brave and modest man, to face the inevitable, and will resign himself to Heaven, as one does to a great function from which exclusion would be a social disgrace, to which admission is a joyless honour. Certainly this man is not a St. John, but it does not follow that he is quite hopeless. The conventional heaven is antipathetic to him not because he is unspiritual but because he is natural.

It must also strike one that an office of devotion would be an inept and disappointing conclusion to the present life. For what purpose are we placed and kept in this world? Faith answers, in order that we may be educated for the life to come : this is how Faith solves the perplexing problem of the life which now is. Providence endows a person with some natural gift, arranges that this gift be developed, affords it a field of exercise, trains it within sight of perfection. There is something which this person can do better than his fellows, and that is his capital for future enterprise. Two possessions we shall carry with us into the unseen : they are free of death, and inalienable—one is character, the other is capacity. Is this capacity to be consigned to idleness and wantonly wasted? It were unreason : it were almost a crime. How this or that gift can be utilised in the other world is a vain question, and leads to childish speculation. We do not know where the unseen universe is, nor how it is constituted, much less how it is ordered, but our reason may safely conclude that the capacity which is exercised under one form here will be exercised under another yonder. 'It is surely a frivolous notion,' says Isaac Taylor, that the vast and intricate machinery of the universe, and the profound scheme of God's government, are now to reach a resting place, where nothing more shall remain to active spirits through an eternity but recollections of labour, anthems of praise, and inert repose.'

This uninviting Heaven owes its imagination to two causes—the tradition of asceticism and an abuse of the Apocalypse. Fantastic ideas of religion, which were reared under monastic glass, have been acclimatised in certain schools, whose favoured doctrines have no analogy in life, and whose cherished ideals make no appeal to the heart. Sensible people agree that character is the pledge of goodness, and that work is a condition of happiness, and that a sphere where good men could do their work without weariness in the light of God's face would be an ideal heaven, but sensible people are apt to be brow-beaten by traditions and to say what is not real. Unfortunately a really preposterous

Paradise has been also credited with the glory of St. John's new Jerusalem, which cometh down 'from God . . . as a bride adorned for her husband,' whose foundations were 'garnished with all manner of precious stones,' whose street was 'pure gold, as it were transparent glass.' This is the vision of a Jewish mystic, very splendid poetry to be read for the sound and beauty thereof, and they are not to be lightly forgiven who have reduced it to bathos in certain pictures and books. St. John imagined the kingdom of Jesus in its glory moving like a stately harmony before the eyes of God, and cast his imagination into the ancient symbols of Jewish literature. He intended the age of gold.

Any view of the future may be fairly tried by this criterion—does it strengthen, gladden, inspire us in the present? Whenever this question is put, we turn to Jesus with His doctrine of continuity. Where the traditional forecast fails is in the absence of Hope. It takes all purpose from our present effort, whose hard-won gains in service are to be flung away. It takes all opportunity from the future, which is to be a state of practical inertia. It is the depreciation of the market-place, the workshop, the study; it is the vindication of a Trappist monastery. Where the forecast of Jesus tells is in the spirit of Hope; it invests the most trivial or sordid details of this life with significance, changing them into the elementary exercises of a great science; it points to the future as the heights of life to which we are climbing out of this narrow valley. One of the most pathetic sights in this life is to see a dying man struggling to the last in his calling, putting another touch to his unfinished picture, adding another page to his half-written book. 'Art is long; life is short' comes to our mind, but how stands the case? If the monkish heaven be true, then this foolish mortal had better be done with art or letters, for they can have no place in the land to which he hasteth. If Jesus' heaven be true, then he is bound to gather the last penny of interest on his talents, and make himself fit for his new work. Jesus heartens His followers by an assurance that not one hour of labour, not one grain of attainment, not one honest effort on to the moment when the tools of earth drop from their hands, but will tell on the after life. Again, one is tempted to quote the sagacious Taylor : 'All the practical skill we acquire in managing affairs, all the versatility, the sagacity, the calculation of chances, the patience and assiduity, the promptitude and facility, as well as the highest virtues, which we are learning every day, may well find scope in a world such as is rationally anticipated when we think of heaven as the stage of life which is next to follow the discipline of life.'

It follows upon Jesus' suggestion of the next life,—the continuation of the present on a higher level,—that it will be itself a continual progress, and Jesus gives us frequent hints of this law.   When He referred to the many mansions in His Father's house, He may have been intending rooms—places where those who had been associated together on earth may be gathered together; but He may be rather intending stations—stages in that long ascent of life that shall extend through the ages of ages. In the parable of the unjust steward Jesus uses this expression in speaking of the future, 'everlasting tents.'   It is at once a contradiction and an explanation, for it combines the ideas of rest and advance—a life of achievement, where the tent is pitched, a life of possibilities, where it is being for ever lifted.

> ' Will the future life be work,
>   Where the strong and the weak, this world's congeries,
>   Repeat in large what they practised in small,
>   Through life after life in unlimited series,
>   Only the scales be changed, that's all ? '

Does not this conception of the future solve a very dark problem—the lives that have never arrived.   Beside the man whose gifts have been laid out at usury and gained a splendid interest, are others whose talents have been hid, not by their own doing, but by Providence.   They realised their gift; they cherished it; they would have used it; but for them there was no market.   Providence, who gave them wings, placed them in a cage.   Round us on every side are cramped, hindered, still-born lives—merchants who should have been painters, clerks who should have been poets, labourers who should have been philosophers.   Their talent is known to a few friends; they die, and the talent is buried in their coffin.   Jesus says No.   It has at last been sown for the harvest; it will come into the open and blossom in another land. These also are being trained—trained by wait-

ing. They are the reserve of the race, kept behind the hill till God requires it. They will get
their chance ; they will come into their kingdom,

> ' Where the days bury their golden suns
> In the dear hopeful West.'

The continuity of life lifts the shadow also
from another mystery—the lives that have been
cut off in their prime. When one is richly endowed and carefully trained, and has come to
the zenith of his power, his sudden removal
seems a reflection on the economy of God's
kingdom. Why call this man to the choir
celestial when he is so much needed in active
service? According to Jesus, he has not sunk
into inaction, so much subtracted from the
forces of righteousness. He has gone where
the fetters of this body of humiliation and em-
barrassment of adverse circumstances shall be
no longer felt. We must not think of him as
withdrawn from the field; we must imagine
him as in the van of battle. We must follow
him, our friend, with hope and a high heart.

> ' No, at noon-day, in the bustle of man's worktime,
> Greet the unseen with a cheer ;
> Bid him forward breast and back as either should be,
> " Strive and thrive," cry " speed, fight on, fare ever
> There as here !" '

THE KINGDOM OF GOD

THE KINGDOM OF GOD

THE KINGDOM OF GOD

THE KINGDOM OF GOD

There are times when one wishes he had never read the New Testament Scriptures— that he might some day open St. Luke's Gospel, and the most beautiful book in the world might come upon his soul like sunrise. It is a doubtful fortune to be born in Athens and every day to see the Parthenon against the violet sky: better to make a single pilgrimage and carry forever the vision of beauty in your heart. Devout Christians must be haunted by the fear that Jesus' sublime words may have lost their heavenliness through our familiarity, or that they may have been overlaid by our conventional interpretations. This misgiving is confirmed by the fact that from time to time a fresh discovery is made in Jesus' teaching. As a stranger, unfettered by tradition, will detect in a private gallery some masterpiece gen-

erations have overlooked, so an unbiassed
mind will rescue from neglecting ages some
idea of the Master. Two finds have been made
within recent years: the Divine Fatherhood
and the Kingdom of God.

If any one will take the three Gospels and
read them with an open ear, he will be amazed
by the continual recurrence of this phrase, the
' Kingdom of God ' or ' Heaven.' Jesus is ever
preaching the Kingdom of God and explaining
it in parables and images of exquisite simplicity. He exhorts men to make any sacrifice that
they may enter the Kingdom of God. He
warns certain that they must not look back lest
they should not be fit for the Kingdom of God.
He declares that it is not possible for others to
enter the Kingdom of God. He encourages
some one because he is not far from the Kingdom of God. He gives to His chief Apostle
the keys of the Kingdom of Heaven. He
rates the Pharisees because they shut up the
Kingdom of Heaven against men. He com-
forts the poor because theirs is the Kingdom
of Heaven; and He invites the nations to sit
down with Abraham in the Kingdom of
Heaven. The Kingdom was in His thought

the chiefest good of the soul and the hope of
the world.

> ' One far-off divine event
> To which the whole creation moves.'

Every prophet of the first order has his own
message and it crystalises into a favourite idea.
With Moses the ruling idea was law; with
Confucius, it was morality; with Buddha, it
was Renunciation; with Mohammed, it was
God; with Socrates, it was the Soul. With
the Master, it was the Kingdom of God. The
idea owed its origin to the Theocracy, its inspiration to Isaiah, its form to Daniel, its popu-
larity to John Baptist. When the forerunner's
voice was stifled in the dungeon of Herod,
Jesus caught up his word and preached the
Utopia of John with a wider vision and
sweeter note. The hereditary dream of the
Jew passed through the soul of Jesus and was
transformed. The local widened into the universal; the material was raised to the spiritual.
A Jewish state with Jerusalem for its capital,
and a greater David for its king, changed at
the touch of Jesus into a moral kingdom whose
throne should be in the heart and its borders
conterminous with the race. The largeness of

Jesus' mind is its glory and its misfortune. The magnificent conception was refused by his countrymen because their God was a national Deity; it has been too often reduced by His disciples because they have no horizon. They have been apt to think that Christianity is an extremely clever scheme by which a limited number 'of souls will secure Heaven—a rocket apparatus for a shipwrecked crew. Perhaps therefore outside people should be excused for speaking of Christianity as a system of the higher selfishness, because they have some grounds for their misunderstanding. Every one ought to read Jesus' own words and he would find that Jesus did not live and die to afford select Pharisees an immunity from the burden of their fellow-men, but to found a Kingdom that would be the salvation of the world.

It has been a calamity that for long Christians paid hardly any attention to the idea of the Kingdom of Jesus on which He was always insisting, and gave their whole mind to the entirely different idea of the Church, which Jesus only mentioned once with intention in a passage of immense difficulty. The Kingdom-

idea flourishes in every corner of the three
Gospels, and languishes in the Acts and Epistles, while the Church-idea is practically non-
existent in Jesus' sermons, but saturates the
letters of St. Paul.   This means that the idea
which unites has been forgotten, the idea which
separates has been magnified.   With all respect
to the ablest Apostle of Jesus, one may be allowed to express his regret that St. Paul had
not said less about the Church and more about
the Kingdom.   One gratefully acknowledges
St. Paul's own mystical idea of the Church, also
one knows why the Church has a stronger fascination for the ordinary religious person than
the Kingdom.   With him the Church is a
visible and exclusive institution which men can
manage and use.   The Kingdom is a spiritual
and inclusive society whose members are selected by natural fitness and which is beyond
human control.   One must *affirm* this or that
to be a member of the Church; one must *be*
something to be a part of the Kingdom of God.
Every person who is like Christ in character, or
is of His mind, is included in the Kingdom.
No natural reading of Church can include
Plato: no natural reading of Kingdom can

322 THE MIND OF THE MASTER

exclude him. The effect of the two institutions upon the world is a contrast. The characteristic product of the Church is ecclesiastics; the characteristic product of the Kingdom is philanthropists.

Jesus' Kingdom commends itself to the imagination because it is to come, when God's will is done on earth as it is done in heaven—it is the Kingdom of the Beatitudes. It commends itself to the reason because it has come wherever any one is attempting God's will—it is the Kingdom of the Parables. An ideal state, it ever allures and inspires its subjects; a real state, it sustains, commands them. Had Jesus conceived His Kingdom as in the future only, He had made His disciples dreamers; had He centred it in the present only, He had made them theorists. As it is, one labours on its building with a splendid model before his eyes; one possesses it in his heart, and yet is ever entering into its fulness. When Jesus sat down with the twelve in the upper room, the Kingdom of God had come; when the Son of Man shall be seen 'coming in a cloud with power and great glory' it shall be 'nigh at hand.' As Jesus came once and ever cometh, so His Kingdom is a present fact and an endless hope.

Jesus commands attention and respect at once when He insisted on a present Kingdom. It was not going to be, it was now and here. That very day a man could see, could enter, could possess, could serve the Kingdom of God. Jesus did not despise this world in which we live nor despair of human society to which we belong. He did not discount earth in favour of heaven nor make the life which now is a mere passage to rest. He deliberately founded His Kingdom in this world, and anticipated it would run its course amid present circumstances. If you had pointed to rival forces and opposing interests, Jesus accepted the risk. If sin and selfishness had their very seat here, then the more need for the counteraction of the Kingdom. In fact, if there is to be a kingdom of God anywhere, it must be in this world ; and if it be impossible here where Jesus died, it will be impossible in Mars or anywhere. When Jesus said the Kingdom of Heaven, be sure He did not mean an unseen refuge whither a handful might one day escape like persecuted and disheartened Puritans fleeing from a hopeless England, but He intended what might be and then was in Galilee, what should be and now is in England. 'To those who speak to you of heaven and seek to separate it from earth,' wrote Mazzini, 'you will say that heaven and earth are one even as the way and the goal are one.' And he used also to say, and his words are coming true before our eyes, 'The first real faith that shall arise upon the ruins of the old worn-out creeds will transform the whole of our actual social organisation, because the whole history of humanity is but the repetition in form and degree of the Christian prayer, "Thy kingdom come: Thy will be done on earth as it is in heaven."'

Jesus' next point is that the Kingdom consists of regenerate individuals, and therefore He was always trying to create character. This is the salient difference between Jesus and the Jewish reformers and all reformers. The reformer, who has his own function and is to be heartily commended, approaches humanity from the outside and proceeds by machinery; Jesus approaches humanity from the inside and proceeds by influence. No one can ask a question without at the same time revealing his mind ; and so when the Pharisees demanded of Jesus when the Kingdom of God should come, one understands what was their method of social reformation.   The new state of things which they called the Kingdom of God—and no better name for Utopia has ever been found—was to come with observation.   It was to be a sudden demonstration, and behold the golden age has begun.   What they exactly meant was the arrival of a viceroy from God endowed with supernatural power and authority.   Till He came, patriotism could do nothing ; when He came, patriotism would simply obey, and in a day the hopes of the saints would be realised and the promises of the prophets fulfilled.   At one blow the Roman grip would be loosened from the throat of the Jewish nation ; the grinding bondage of taxation swept away; the insolent license of Herod's court ended ; the pride of the priestly aristocracy reduced, and the gross abuses of the temple worship redressed.   When the Messiah came, they would see the ideal of patriotism in all ages : ' A Free State and a Free Church.' It was a splendid dream, the idea of a ready-made commonwealth, that has touched in turn and glorified Savonarola and Sir Thomas More, Scottish Covenanters and English Puritans, and inspired the noblest minds in Greece. It is that society can be regenerated from without and in the mass! It is regeneration by machinery—very magnificent machinery no doubt, but still machinery.

Jesus believed that if the Kingdom of God is to come at all, it must be by another method, and it was the perpetual exposition of His method that brought Him into collision with the Pharisees. He knew that the Messiah for the Jews must not be a supernatural Roman emperor or a *Deus ex machinâ*, doing for men what they would not do for themselves. This Messiah was a moral impossibility and this paternal Government would be useless. The true Messiah was a Saviour who would hold up a personal ideal and stimulate men to fulfil it. What was any nation but three measures of meal to be leavened; you must leaven it particle by particle till it be all changed. Instead of looking hither and thither for the Kingdom of God it would be better to look for it in men's own hearts and lives. The Pharisees prated about being free, meaning they had certain political privileges; but Jesus told them that the highest liberty was freedom from sin. Did a Pharisee—and the Pharisee with all his faults was the patriot of his day—desire to better his nation; then let him begin by bettering himself. When the Pharisees learned humility and sympathy, the golden age would not be far distant from Jewry. Jesus' perpetual suggestion to the patriotic class of His day was that they should turn from the politics of the state to the ethics of their own lives.

Jesus afforded a standing illustration of His own advice by His marked abstention from politics. His attitude is not only unexpected, it is amazing and perplexing. He never said one word against the Roman domination; He was on cordial terms with Roman officers; He cast His shield over the hated publican; He tolerated even Herod and Pilate. This was not an accident; it was His line. When clever tacticians laid a trap for Him and pressed Him for a confession of His political creed, He escaped by telling them He had none. Some things were civic, some religious. Let each sphere be kept apart. 'Render unto Cæsar the things which are Cæsar's, and unto God the

things which are God's :' as for Him, His concern was with divine things. Jesus was so
guarded that He refused to arbitrate in a dispute about property—a duty now greedily un-
dertaken by His servants. When He stood
before Pilate, on the day of the cross, He told
that bewildered officer that His kingdom was
not of this world, and did not give him the
slightest help in arranging a compromise.

On the other hand, none can read Jesus'
words without being perfectly certain that they
must sooner or later change the trend of politics and the colour of the state. His contempt-
uous depreciation of the world, His solemn
appreciation of the soul, His sense of the
danger of riches, His doctrine of the Fatherhood of God, His sympathy with the poor, His
enthusiasm of humanity, were not likely to return unto Him void. No man can read Jesus'
Sermon on the Mount or His parables—largely
taken from the sphere of labour—or His arguments with the Pharisees, without being leavened with new and unworldly ideas. When
these ideas have taken hold of the mind, they
will be carried as principles of action into the
state. Moral truths ripen slowly; but given

time, and Christianity was bound to become
the most potent force in the state, although
Jesus had never said one word about politics,
and His apostles had adhered closely to His
example. Men who have been fed with
Christ's bread, and in whose heart His spirit is
striving, will not long tolerate slavery, tyranny,
vice, or ignorance. If they do not apply the
principle to the fact to-day, they will to-
morrow. Their conscience is helpless in the
grip of Christ's word. They will be con-
strained to labour in the cause of Christ, and
when their work is done men will praise them.
It is right that they should receive their crown,
but the glory does not belong to Hampden
and Howard and Wilberforce and Shaftesbury
and Lincoln and Gordon; it belongs to Jesus,
who stood behind these great souls and inspired them. He never assailed Pilate with
bitter invective, or any other person, except religious hypocrites; He never hinted at an in-
surrection. But it is Jesus, more than any
other man or force, that has made Pilates impossible, and taught the human race to live
and die for freedom.

Politics are after all only a necessary machinery; what comes first is ideas. Just as there is the physical which we see and handle, and the metaphysical which eye has not seen nor ear heard, so there is the political, which takes shape in government and legislatures and laws, and there is the meta-political—to use a happy phrase in *Lux Mundi*—which is before all and above all, or politics are worthless. And just as no wise physicist rails at the metaphysical because it cannot be weighed in scales, but freely acknowledges that it is the spirit of the material, so every one knows that all worthy politics are the offspring of noble ideas. When Jesus denied Himself to politics, He did not abdicate His Kingdom; He set up His throne above all the world-kingdoms and entrenched it among the principles that judge and govern life. When He declined to agitate, He did not abandon the people. He could not, for, unlike many of their pseudo-friends, Jesus loved the people unto death. But He had a wide horizon. He was not content to change their circumstances, He dared to attempt something higher—to change their souls.

Had Jesus depended on a scheme rather than an influence, He had failed. Imagine if He had anticipated the fruits of Christianity, and asked the world to accept the emancipation of the slave and the equality of woman, and civil rights and religious liberty, Christianity would have been crushed at its birth. It would have spelled anarchy, and in that day would have been anarchy. With the slow, sure education of centuries, these changes have come to be synonymous with righteousness. Christianity may be to-day pregnant with changes for which we are not prepared. They will come to birth bye-and-bye and find people prepared for them. What to our fathers would have seemed a revolution will seem to our children a regeneration. A century ago a slave-owner would have defended himself from God's Word, to-day he would be cast headlong out of the Church. Yesterday a master sweated his servants without sense of wrong-doing, to-day he is ashamed. To-day a millionaire is respected; there are signs that in future years a man leaving a huge fortune will be thought a semi-criminal. So does the Spirit of Jesus spread and ferment. Christ did not ask for power to make laws, He asked for a few men to train—for soil in which to sow His truth. He was content to wait till a generation arose, and said, ' Before God this must be done,' and then it would be done as Jesus intended. Possess the imagination with an ideal, and one need not vex himself about action.

Jesus laid Himself alongside sinful people, and out of them He slowly built up the new kingdom. If a man was a formalist, he must be born again ; if the slave of riches, he must sell all he had ; if in the toils of a darling sin, he must pluck out his right eye to enter the kingdom of God. New men to make a new state. The kingdom was humility, purity, generosity, unselfishness. It was the reign of character; it was the struggle for perfection. Chunder Sen, the Indian prophet, described Jesus' Kingdom perfectly : ' A spiritual congregation of souls born anew to God.' Say not, ' Lo here, lo there,' as if one could see a system or a government. 'The kingdom of God is within you.'

Investigate a little farther, and you notice that Jesus fused His disciples into one body, and, by this act alone, separated Himself from the method of philosophy. Philosophy is content with an audience ; Jesus demands a society.   Philosophy teaches men to think ; Jesus moves them to do.   Philosophy can do no more because it has no centre of unity : the kingdom of God is richer, for there is Jesus.   Socrates obliterated himself ; Jesus asserted Himself, and united His followers to each other by binding them to Himself.   Loyalty to Jesus was to be the spinal cord to the new body, and the sacraments were to be the signs of the new spirit.   Each was perfect in its simplicity—a beautiful poem.   One was Baptism, where the candidate for God's kingdom disappeared into water and appeared again with another name. This meant that he had died to self and had risen a new creature, the child of the Divine Will.   The other was the Lord's Supper, where Jesus' disciple eats bread and drinks wine in remembrance of His death.   This meant that he had entered into the spirit of his Master and given himself to the service of the world. Those are the only rites of Jesus, those His bonds, and with this lowly equipment—two pledges of sacrifice—began the Kingdom of God.   Within all nations, and under the shadow of all governments, dividing none, resisting none, winning all and uniting all, was to rise the new state of peace and goodwill toward men.

How was the kingdom to impress itself upon the world and change the colour of human life? As Jesus did Himself, and after no other fashion. Of all conquerors He has had the highest ambition, and above them all He has seen His desire. He has dared to demand men's hearts as well as their lives and has won them —how? By coercion? by stratagem? by cleverness? by splendour? By none of those means that have been used by rules. By a scheme of his own invention—by the Cross. The Cross meant the last devotion to humanity; it was the pledge of the most uncomplaining and effectual ministry. When you inquire the resources of the Kingdom of Heaven, behold the Cross. They are faith and love. Its soldiers are the humble, the meek, the gentle, the peaceful. 'Forgive your enemies,' said Jesus; 'help the miserable, restore the fallen, set the captive free. Love as I have loved, and you will succeed.' Amazing simplicity! amazing originality! Hitherto kingdoms had stood on the principle of selfishness—grasp and keep. This kingdom was to rest on sacrifice—suffer and serve. Amazing hope, that anything so weak, so helpless, could regenerate the masterful world! But Jesus has not been put to shame: His plan has not failed. There are many empires on the face of the earth to-day, but none so dominant as the kingdom of God. Jesus by the one felicitous stroke of the Cross has replaced the rule of rights by the idea of sacrifice; and when Jesus' mind has obtained everywhere, and the men cease to ask, 'What am I to get,' and begin to say, 'What can I give,' then we shall see a new heaven and a new earth wherein dwelleth righteousness.

It was natural that the imagination of Jesus should inspire heroic souls in every age; it was perhaps inevitable that few could enter into His mind. Nothing has given such a moral impetus to human society; nothing has conferred such nobility of character as the Kingdom of God; nothing has been so sadly misunderstood. The sublime self-restraint of Jesus, His inexhaustible patience, His immovable charity, His unerring insight, did not descend to certain of His disciples. They longed to anticipate the victory of righteousness, and burned to cleanse the world by force. Such eager souls gained for themselves an imperishable name, but they failed. When the Roman Empire was laid waste, and the world seemed to be falling to pieces, St. Augustine described the new empire that should rise on the ashes of the old. The *City of God* stands first among his writings, and created the Holy Roman Empire, but the Papacy has not redeemed humanity. When the life of Florence was eaten out by the Medicis, Savonarola purified the city for a space with a thunderstorm. The Florentines cast out their Herods at the bidding of their Baptist, they burned their vanities in the market-place, they elected Jesus King of Florence by acclamation. In a little they brought Herod back, and burned the Baptist in the same market-place. The Puritans were at first quiet, serious, peaceable men who were outraged by the reign of unrighteousness, and drew the sword to deliver England. They made the host of God triumphant for a little. Then came the reaction, and iniquity covered the land as with a flood. It was high failure, but

it was failure.   It does not become us to criticise those forlorn hopes; we ought to learn
from their reverses.   The Kingdom of God can
only rule over willing hearts ; it has no helots
within its borders.   It advances by individual
conversion, it stands in individual consecration.
Laws can do but little for this cause; the sword
less than nothing.   The kingdom will come in
a land when it has come in the hearts of the
people—neither sooner nor later.

The Kingdom of God cometh to a man when
he sets up Jesus' Cross in his heart, and begins
to live what Mr. Laurence Oliphant used to
call 'the life.'   It passes on its way when that
man rises from table and girds himself and
serves the person next him.   Yesterday the
kingdom was one man; now it is a group.
From the one who washes to the one whose
feet are washed the kingdom grows and multi-
plies.   It stands around us on every side,—
not in Pharisees nor in fanatics, not in noise
nor tumult, but in modest and Christ-like men.
One can see it in their faces, and catch it in the
tone of their voices.   And if one has eyes to
see and ears to hear, then let him be of good

Y

cheer, for the Kingdom of God is come.   It is the world-wide state, whose law is the Divine will, whose members obey the spirit of Jesus, whose strength is goodness, whose heritage is God.

THE END.